WRITINGS FROM
The New Yorker
1927–1976

Books by E. B. White

Poems and Sketches of E. B. White
Essays of E. B. White
Letters of E. B. White
The Trumpet of the Swan
The Points of My Compass
The Second Tree From the Corner
Charlotte's Web
Here Is New York
The Wild Flag
Stuart Little
One Man's Meat
The Fox of Peapack
Quo Vadimus?
Farewell to Model T
Every Day Is Saturday
The Lady Is Cold

E. B. WHITE

WRITINGS FROM
The New Yorker
1927–1976

Edited by Rebecca M. Dale

HarperCollins*Publishers*

WRITINGS FROM *THE NEW YORKER*. Copyright © 1990 by Joel White and Rebecca Dale. Introduction and Bibliography copyright © 1990 by Rebecca Dale. All rights reserved. Printed in the United States of America. No part of this book may be used or reproduced in any manner whatsoever without written permission except in the case of brief quotations embodied in critical articles and reviews. For information address HarperCollins Publishers, 10 East 53rd Street, New York, N.Y. 10022.

Designed by Karen Savary

Library of Congress Cataloging-in-Publication Data

White, E. B. (Elwyn Brooks), 1899–1985
    Writings from the New Yorker / E.B. White.—1st ed.
      p. cm.
    ISBN 0-06-016517-0
    I. New Yorker. II. Title.
PS3545.H5187A6   1990
814'.52—dc20   89-46564

    91 92 93 94 CC/HC 10 9 8 7 6 5 4 3 2

CONTENTS

INTRODUCTION

While working on an independent study project at Virginia Commonwealth University in 1988, reading all of E. B. White's *New Yorker* work, I kept discovering many delightful pieces of prose that had never been collected in any of his books. This collection presents some of that work.

E. B. White is perhaps best known for his children's books *(Stuart Little, Charlotte's Web, The Trumpet of the Swan),* but he was primarily a writer for *The New Yorker,* where he wrote anonymously "Notes and Comment," "Talk of the Town," and newsbreaks, those fillers at the end of articles with wry comments on clippings from newspapers and magazines. He began sending contributions to *The New Yorker* in 1925 and writing "Notes and Comment" for it in 1926. When White moved to Maine in 1938, he started writing a monthly column, "One Man's Meat," for *Harper's Magazine* and he wrote only occasionally for *The New Yorker.* After resigning from *Harper's* in 1943, he resumed writing frequently for *The New Yorker.* The Whites divided their time between New York and Maine from 1943 until 1957, when they moved permanently to their home in Maine. He died in 1985 at the age of 86.

In his *New Yorker* work, White commented on the news and people of the time, connecting them to broader concerns. He embraced the themes he noted as Thoreau's, "man's relation to Nature and man's dilemma in society and man's capacity for elevating his spirit," and, like Thoreau, "beat all these matters together," producing "an original omelette from which people can draw nourishment in a hungry day" ("A Slight Sound at Evening," *Essays of E. B. White*). Like Thoreau, White delighted in exploring the fullness of life as an individual. Like Thoreau, he was divided between "the desire to enjoy the world (and not be derailed by a mosquito wing) and the urge to set the world straight." Moreover, White, unlike Thoreau, felt an empathic bond with humanity, a certain bond with others that Thoreau did not feel. While he was often playful in his writing, sometimes delighting in the spirit of fun for its own sake, he also dealt with important subjects, and his writing is often quite lyrical—poetry in prose form. His humor, which permeated nearly all of his writing, is the type that "plays close to the big hot fire which is Truth" ("Some Remarks on Humor," *Essays*). As we read White's work in its variety of moods, we experience his vitality, his subtle irony, his gentle but pointed satire, his unpretentious manner and admiration of simplicity, his spirit of fun, and his compassion and concern.

The pieces presented here were selected and arranged by the White family from selections and arrangements I proposed for this collection. The pieces are in roughly chronological order within each part to show a historical perspective on the United States from the Depression years through World War II and the postwar years, the evolution of *The New Yorker*'s editorial concerns, the development of E. B. White as a writer from his young voice and early promise to his more assured work and weightier subjects, and, over the years, his increasing refinement of writing style and humor.

The early pieces (twenties and thirties) examine life's little adversities and are short, frothy, witty, even sometimes flippant. The later pieces (from the forties on) are less whimsical and focus on more serious matters such as liberty, international affairs, and the environment, but even these have his graceful touch of humor. White's pieces became longer and more intricate structurally in the fifties; most of his long essays have been collected in *Essays of E. B. White*, which makes a good companion to this collection.

Most of the pieces are excerpts from "Notes and Comment," each piece bearing the date of its publication in *The New Yorker* and transcribed as it was printed in the magazine. Because "Notes and Comment" was an editorial column, White had to follow magazine policy of using "we" instead of "I." He disliked the awkwardness of the practice, saying it gave "the impression that the stuff was written by a set of identical twins or the members of a tumbling act" (Foreword, *The Second Tree from the Corner*). Despite White's preference for "I" over "we," I have not altered any of his words from the text as it appeared in *The New Yorker*. The footnotes are editorial additions; I have tried to keep them to a minimum.

Many of White's *New Yorker* and *Harper*'s pieces are collected in his previously published books. His collected work, even counting this collection, contains only a small portion of the hundreds of paragraphs and essays he wrote over the years. Katherine Hall's *E. B. White: A Bibliographical Catalogue* lists 450 signed pieces and 1350 identifiable unsigned columns in *The New Yorker* from 1925 to 1976, the last year he contributed a piece (the one titled "A Busy Place" in this collection). Her bibliography is based on manuscripts White donated to Cornell University's Olin Library and on a scrapbook of his articles in various magazines put together and donated to the library by Scott Elledge, professor of English at Cornell and White's biographer. Elledge, in turn, relied on the White scrapbooks in the files at *The New Yorker*, which are the basic source for identifying which parts of the unsigned columns are White's work.

Ebba Johnson, head librarian at *The New Yorker* from 1934 to 1970, now deceased, and Helen Stark, the current librarian, deserve appreciation as the curators of those White scrapbooks. I also thank Katherine Hall, who, in her bibliography, has made information on White's work readily available. I thank Bryant Mangum, Bill Griffin, and Terry Oggel of Virginia Commonwealth University for their advice to me on this project, and I thank my family for their support. In putting together this collection, I tried to imagine how E. B. White would have wanted it done. I relied on his family and Cass Canfield, Jr., of HarperCollins (the son of his editor at Harper & Row) for advice, and I appreciate their suggestions and enthusiasm for the project. Although White is not here to speak for himself, he deserves to have the last word. In a note in Hall's bibliography concerning "Notes and Comment," he wrote how he came up with ideas for the column: "People on the staff and other people who were readers of the magazine used to submit comment ideas, and I always had a folder of these ideas and suggestions on my desk, together with clippings and stuff that I would toss into the folder from my own reading." He wished to acknowledge these "thousand mysterious and unremembered sources."

Rebecca M. Dale
1990

1

Nature

LIFE

AT EIGHT OF A HOT MORNING, the cicada speaks his first piece. He says of the world: heat. At eleven of the same day, still singing, he has not changed his note but has enlarged his theme. He says of the morning: love. In the sultry middle of the afternoon, when the sadness of love and of heat has shaken him, his symphonic soul goes into the great movement and he says: death. But the thing isn't over. After supper he weaves heat, love, death into a final stanza, subtler and less brassy than the others. He has one last heroic monosyllable at his command. Life, he says, reminiscing. Life.

PROHIBITED

THE PLANT-PATENT BUSINESS is taking right hold, apparently. We know a man who received a birthday present of a nice little azalea. Tied around the azalea's stem, like a chastity belt, was a metal tag from Bobbink & Atkins, reading, "Asexual reproduction of this plant is illegal under the Plant Patent Act." It was Number 147. Our friend, a man of loose personal habits, ripped the tag off angrily, fed it to his dachshund puppy, and sent the plant to a friend in Connecticut with instructions to bed it down warmly next to an old buck hydrangea.

SUMMERTIME

8/12/44

SUMMERTIME THIS YEAR is a ripe girl who finds herself forsaken by the boys, the ordinarily attentive and desirous boys. They are nowhere to be found; they have disappeared, the way males do, seized by some sudden mechanical flirtation, some new interest of a passing sort. Summertime is a girl who knows they will be back and who is conscious that she herself is irresistible over the long term, that her beauty and her accommodating ways have lost no fraction of their power. We had summertime practically to ourself the other afternoon, and in our guilt we lay with her in the name of all who were temporarily denied that privilege, admiring her incredible poise. The scent of her clothes was unmistakable; her sea, her sand, her sky wore the same look as ever; the insects which are her private minstrels sang the same seductive measure. We have never seen a discarded female more sure of where she stood than summertime.

SEEDS

1/12/52

OUR FIRST COMMUNICATION of the year 1952 was a card from a seed company, and this seemed a good omen. A new bush bean, rich in flavor. A new pickle, early, dark green, delicious. A new muskmelon, thick orange flesh of top quality. A new petunia, giant fringed, dwarfish. So starts the year on a note of planning and dreaming. The card went on to chide us—said no order had been received from us since 1949. That is a fantastic accusation; we virtually supported that seed house last year and the year before and the year before, back into the dim, infertile past. However, we don't expect seed companies

4

to keep accurate records; the whole business is so wild, so riotous, so complex, it's no wonder they forget who their own best friends are. If there is any doubt on that score, though, we will gladly send the management a jar of our wife's green-tomato pickle from last summer's crop—dark green, spicy, delicious, costlier than pearls when you figure the overhead.

DRESSING UP

4/20/46

ONE OF THE MALE SPARROWS in Turtle Bay garden made a wonderful discovery at quarter past nine the other morning. He found a small length of blue confetti tied in a bow. The morning was springlike, although a trifle cool, and the combination of blue confetti and blue sky stirred him up. He carried his find to the branch of a large sycamore, where he sat waiting to be photographed. (It really looked as though he had on an outsize Windsor tie.) After a minute or two, he moved on to a willow, then to Dorothy Thompson's gate, then to an ailanthus. Pretty soon the word got around and other sparrows of both sexes showed up, the ladies to admire, the men to jeer. It was fairly obvious that the owner of the blue bow tie was uncertain about his next move. He was undecided whether to start nest building, using a blue confetti bow tie as a sill piece (and face all the involvements and commitments that follow nest building), or whether just to wear the damned thing. He unquestionably was enjoying the fuss, and when the attention of the other birds flagged, he purposely dropped the bow, allowed it to spiral down almost to the fountain, then swooped and recovered it in midair. This drew a round of applause. We watched the act for twenty minutes, at the end of which time the sparrow dropped the bow again and flew away to a neighborhood saloon. It is a wearisome thing to be overdressed in the early morning.

TOMORROW SNOW

3/20/48

ALONE OVER A WEAKFISH in the deep noonday shadows of the Roosevelt Grill, we spelled out the strong editorials in the *News,* occasionally lighting a match to read some of the more challenging passages. Our waiter drifted over after a while and stood quietly at our side. "It's so beautiful," he murmured. "What is, Father?" we asked. "This day, this perfect soft spring day." He pointed east, where the faint luminosity of Vanderbilt Avenue showed through the blinds and gave the restaurant a ribbon of golden light. His voice had tears in it. "I've been listening to the radio," he said. "Tomorrow snow, turning to rain." He was a man carrying foreknowledge in his breast, and the pain was almost unbearable. We don't remember a winter when people followed the elements so closely and when foreknowledge so completely destroyed any chance of momentary bliss.

DISMAL?

2/25/50

THE MOST STARTLING NEWS in the paper on February 13th was the weather forecast. It was "Rainy and dismal." When we read the word "dismal" in the *Times,* we knew that the era of pure science was drawing to a close and the day of philosophical science was at hand. (Probably in the nick of time.) Consider what had happened! A meteorologist, whose job was simply to examine the instruments in his observatory, had done a quick switch and had examined the entrails of birds. In his fumbling way he had attempted to predict the impact of the elements on the human spirit. His was a poor attempt, as it turned out, but it was an attempt. There are, of course, no evil days in nature, no *dies mali,* and the forecast plainly showed that the weatherman had been spending his time indoors. To the intimates of rain, no day is dismal, and a dull sky is as plausible as any other. Nevertheless, the forecast indicated that the connection had been reëstablished between nature and scientific man. Now all we need is a meteorologist who has once been soaked to the skin without ill effect. No one can write knowingly of weather who walks bent over on wet days.

THE ARRIVAL OF SPRING

3/28/53

SPRING ALWAYS USED TO ARRIVE in midtown in the window boxes of the Helen Gould Shepard house. Something about the brightness and suddenness of that hyacinthine moment said Spring, something about its central location, too. The other day, we passed the ruins of the Gould house and shed a private tear for olden springtimes. Spring struggles into Manhattan by other routes these days; Rockefeller Center has pretty much taken the occasion over. Rockefeller's is different from Helen Gould's. Less homey. More like Christmas at Lord & Taylor's—beautiful but contrived. One never really knows where one will encounter the first shiver and shine of spring in the city. Often it is not in a flowering plant at all, merely in a certain quality of the light as it strikes the walls. We met ours quite a while back, late one afternoon in February, driving south through the Park; in an instant the light had lengthened and strengthened and bounced from the towers into our system, hitting us as a dram of tonic reaching the stomach, and, lo, it was spring.

7

WINTER BACK YARD

3/24/51

A CITY BACK YARD on many a winter's day is as shabby and unpromising a spot as the eye can rest on: the sour soil, the flaking surfaces of wall and fence, the bare branch, the doom-sprinkled sky. The tone of our back yard this past month, however, has been greatly heightened by the presence of a number of juncos, the dressiest of winter birds. Even the drabbest yard-scape achieves something like elegance when a junco alights in the foreground—a beautifully turned-out little character who looks as though he were on his way to an afternoon wedding.

PLANT THE GARDEN ANYWAY

4/24/54

WE FIND A USEFUL PARABLE in one of the farm journals, whither we turned, hoping to escape for a few moments the ominous headlines of suspicion in the papers. It was a vain hope. The first headline we encountered was "Danger in the Flower Garden." There is enough poison in a single castor bean to kill a person. The seeds of pinks cause vomiting. Sweet-pea seeds contain a poison that can keep a person bedridden for months. The night-blooming jimson has enough power in its leaves to produce delirium. Daffodil bulbs when eaten cause stomach cramps. And in the lily of the valley is a subtle substance that makes the heart slow down. But the conclusion drawn by the writer of the article, chewing absently on a daffodil bulb, was a good one. *We must plant this garden anyway.* Even in the face of such terrors, we must plant this garden. Quite a few prophets and thinkers, these days, are recommending just the opposite. They advise doing away with a garden that produces such dangers. Let's change the seed, they say.

DANBURY FAIR

SOMETHING MUST HAVE GOTTEN INTO US, because we arrived at the Danbury Fair shortly after sun-up on the first day. Nothing much had started. Freaks and crystal-gazers were still asleep in the back seats of old sedans. They slept with their clothes on. Grass in the tents was still green, untrampled.

In the Guernsey barn a calf had been born during the night. A farmhand was teaching it to suck, squirting milk into its stubborn face as it sprawled in the sweet hay. Near the door a bull was having his hair clipped, murder in his eye, murder in the awful muscles of his neck. The electric clippers made a pleasant noise that seemed to go with the good smell of cattle. When the barber was through, a farmboy asked for a hair trim. He would be going into Danbury that night, wanted to look spruce when he winked at the girls. The man cut his hair with the bull clippers. Outside, on the south end of the race course, the overhanging elms still threw long morning shadows on the track as the trotting horses were sent around for a brisk, the drivers hunched over their rumps.

The first day is really the best; you take your ease and see what goes on. The smells, when we arrived, were just starting to taint the air; the food booths were just starting to smear the first layer of terrible grease on their grills; the faces of the prize dolls were just starting to compete with "your chirce of any pretty lamp." A man in a wing collar was raking, with a tiny rake, the eleventh fairway of a tiny golf course. "Make 80 and win a free airplane ride." Madam Drielle, blonde as a birch leaf, stood in the doorway of her tent, yawning—wise with Love, Business, Marriage, Speculation, and Travel, but still a little sleepy. She hated already the faces of the people who hadn't come yet. Everywhere, sprawled on the ground, were the strange and implausible equipment of the concessionaires— things that fitted vaguely and temporarily into other things. In the big produce tent, marvellously juxtaposed, pumpkins of golden yellow, Crane bathtubs of jade green. We lolled comfortably on the running-board of a truck, watching a Holstein bull get his baptism of bluing. It is not every day one sees a bull bathed. A small lad in spectacles holds the ring of his dripping nose, while a red-cheeked washer dips his tail in bluing-water

9

to make it white. Down the midway Betty, the inexplicable freak of nature, 5 tongues, 3 jaws, Truthful, Tangible, Thriving, Come In. In the poultry house, the sawdust soft underfoot, the birds full of dawn song, cocks in fighting trim, and the inquiring geese penetratingly audible.

It was a long, untroubled day. There is nothing like it. Sitting in the grandstand, watching, between trotting races, a trained bear riding a bicycle. All beginnings are wonderful. We rode home in the cool of the evening, wondering what a bear thinks about when he first sees a bicycle.

SAVE THE GRIZZLIES

1/23/32

A COMMITTEE HAS APPROACHED US to ask if we would help in the work of protecting and preserving the brown and grizzly bears of Alaska. Need we say we will? Once we spent six weeks in Alaska, and although we never happened to have an opportunity to protect a grizzly from the predatory old paper-pulp interests, which threaten their extinction, we always stood ready to. We are still ready. The islands of the Inside Passage, where the bears live, seemed to us lovely, perfect. We should not want one of them changed by the extinction of so much as one bear, or the establishment of even one pulp mill. Grizzlies are certainly less dangerous than the tabloids that are printed from paper pulp.

Of course it is our ill fortune always to see both sides of every question. The letter from the Committee on Protection and Preservation of Alaska Brown and Grizzly Bears was written, we notice, on paper. In other words, the Committee are using paper in their campaign against paper pulp. We think they really ought to send out their communications on parchment, preferably made from the hides of sheep especially killed for the purpose by grizzly bears. You see? We're no good in any cause. Too open-minded.

DANISH MOOSE

10/29/49

A DANE TOLD US the other day (and he seemed neither melancholy nor wholly cheerful) that Denmark has two moose.
Denmark used to have only one moose (a bull), but a second
arrived—swam over from Sweden, or took the ferry. The
Danes were worried lest the new arrival prove to be a female.
"Denmark is such a small country; we cannot have it too full
of mooses." The second moose, however, was another bull.
People felt relieved, but they know that it is only a question of
time before some Swedish cow moose learns that there are
extra men south of the border.

ALARM-GEESE

3/21/53

THE MOST STIMULATING PIECE of news we've heard since
Malenkov* came to power is that the British are using geese in
Malaya to fight Communist guerrillas. The geese are employed
as watchdogs, to sound a warning at the approach of the foe.
It happens that we have had quite a good deal to do with geese
in our time, and we feel it advisable to pass along a word of
caution to the British. Geese, we have found, are alert and
articulate and they practically never sleep, but they are also
undiscriminating, gossipy, and as easily diverted as children.
For every alarum they sound to announce a guerrilla, they will
most certainly utter a hundred to announce a British subaltern
who is passing by. Everything and everybody interests a goose,

*Georgi M. Malenkov, Premier of the Soviet Union 1953–55. The British troops
White refers to were stationed in Malaya during the late forties and in the fifties
to fight Chinese Communist guerrillas.

and they play no favorites. Geese have their moods, too, and when geese are in one of their moods, an entire band of guerrillas could walk boldly into camp without stirring up so much as a small greeting. Furthermore, geese sometimes get together and retell old tales, and while at it they make as much noise as though they were announcing the invasion of the planet by little green men. We have an idea that the British will get some real help from geese, but if they feel obliged to act on every report a goose turns in while on duty, they're going to suffer a nervous breakdown into the bargain.

TURTLE BLOOD BANK

1/31/53

WE STROLLED UP TO Hunter College the other evening for a meeting of the New York Zoological Society. Saw movies of grizzly cubs, learned the four methods of locomotion of snakes, and were told that the Society has established a turtle blood bank. Medical men, it seems, are interested in turtle blood, because turtles don't suffer from arteriosclerosis in old age. The doctors are wondering whether there is some special property of turtle blood that prevents the arteries from hardening. It could be, of course. But there is also the possibility that a turtle's blood vessels stay in nice shape because of the way turtles conduct their lives. Turtles rarely pass up a chance to relax in the sun on a partly submerged log. No two turtles ever lunched together with the idea of promoting anything. No turtle ever went around complaining that there is no profit in book publishing except from the subsidiary rights. Turtles do not work day and night to perfect explosive devices that wipe out Pacific islands and eventually render turtles sterile. Turtles never use the word "implementation" or the phrases "hard core" and "in the last analysis." No turtle ever rang another turtle back on the phone. In the last analysis, a turtle, although lacking know-how, knows how to live. A turtle, by its admirable habits, gets to the hard core of life. That may be why its arteries are so soft.

Afterthought: It is worth noting that Chinese do not appear to suffer from arteriosclerosis nearly as much as do Occidentals, and Chinese are heavy eaters of terrapin. Maybe the answer is a double-barrelled one: we should all spend more time on a log in the sun and should eat more turtle soup. With a dash of sherry, of course.

2

The Word

VERMIN

10/7/44

The mouse of Thought infests my head.
He knows my cupboard and the crumb.
    Vermin! I despise vermin.
I have no trap, no skill with traps,
No bait, no hope, no cheese, no bread—
I fumble with the task to no avail.
I've seen him several times lately.
He is too quick for me,
I see only his tail.

THE COST OF HYPHENS

12/15/28

THE PAIN WHICH ATTENDS all literary composition is increased, in some cases, by the writer's knowing how much per word he will receive for his effort. We came upon a writer at his work recently, and were allowed to sit quietly by while he finished his stint. Quite casually he mentioned that he was getting fifty cents a word. A moment or two later his face became contorted with signs of an internal distress. With his hand poised above the machine, he seemed to be fighting something out with himself. Finally he turned to us. "Listen," he said, grimly, "do you hyphenate 'willy-nilly'?" We nodded, and saw him wince as he inserted the little mark, at a cost of half a dollar.

TRAVEL BROCHURE

1/26/35

THE ADVENTURE-MAD TRAVEL-BUREAU PEOPLE run a high fever all the year round, deliriously mumbling of far places regardless of season. More than any other group, they arrange life for us in neat grooves. We have just this moment been skirting through a prospectus of winter and spring trips presented to us by a dutiful and precise agent. The trips are divided into "short" and "long." "There's Mexico," says the booklet. "Ten days, $180." And "there's the Mediterranean, 29 days, $485." Our fancy flits along, jog-step, taking in the sights. And then, as a sudden afterthought, the joyous booklet writer really hits his stride. "There's the WORLD," he cries. "97 days, $833.50."

We had never had the planet laid so neatly at our feet, as though dropped there by a spaniel.

NO VERBS

7/29/39

ON A FETID AFTERNOON LIKE THIS, when all the nobility goes out of a writer and parts of speech lie scattered around the room among cigarette butts and crushed paper cups, we envy the gossip columnists their lot. We particularly envy them their ability to earn a living by talking in participles. You have, of course, observed this phenomenon of the American press—the sentence with no verb. From a literary standpoint it is the prose invention of the century, for it enables the writer to sound as though he were saying something without actually saying it. Thus: "Mrs. Oral Ferrous on the Starlight Roof, chatting with Count de Guiche." Or, "Captain Montmorency Squall, sitting with Mrs. Vincent Trip in a black lace gown and two ropes of pearls." The absence, in these participial items, of any predicate is extremely exciting to the reader, who figures anything might happen. Outside of the columnists, the only person we know who talks entirely in participles is a French-Italian lady who has done our laundry beautifully for years without the use of a single verb. Her sentences don't even have subjects—just participles and adverbs.

It is perhaps only fair to columnists and to the subjects of their stillborn sentences to confess that, a year or more ago, when we discovered that unfinished sentences were having a bad effect on our nerves, we took to completing all sentences under our breath—using a standard predicate. We found that the predicate "ought to be in bed" served well enough, and that is the one we still use. Almost any old predicate will do, however. The important thing is to add it.

WRITER AT WORK

3/26/27

THE WEEK HAS PRODUCED two cases of mortal man's intense itch to see, with his own eyes, a poet or a writer at work. The first case is that of the novelist who will write a book in a glass cage on a Paris boulevard—a chapter every working hour. But the second instance is even more plaintive, richer in human frailty. It concerns our own Edna Millay, who contemplates a trip to Washington. "It would be good," says a Washington news story, "to have this tender poet here in cherry blossom time and to hear her version of this glorious spectacle." (Even the theme is laid out for her, like clean linen.)

MOTIVATION

5/3/30

WHEN HE HEARD ABOUT THE National Arts Club prize for a book which would "reveal the soul of America," one of our dearest friends sat right down and got to work. He had a good plot, and seemed, when we left him, to be much interested in getting it down on paper. When, a day or two later, we saw him again, we were surprised to learn that he had given up the project. It seems that when he read about the prize in the newspaper, he thought it said thirty thousand dollars; later he looked up the clipping and discovered it said three thousand dollars. True to the soul of America, he gave the thing up immediately.

WRITING AS A PROFESSION

5/11/29

"WRITING IS NOT AN OCCUPATION," writes Sherwood Anderson. "When it becomes an occupation a certain amateur spirit is gone out of it. Who wants to lose that?" Nobody does, replies this semi-pro, sitting here straining at his typewriter. Nobody does, yet few writers have the courage to buy a country newspaper, or even to quit a city writing job for anything at all. What Mr. Anderson says is pretty true. Some of the best writings of writers, it seems to us, were done before they actually thought of themselves as engaged in producing literature. Some of the best humor of humorists was produced before ever they heard the distant laughter of their multitudes. Probably what Mr. Anderson means, more specifically, is that life is apt to be translated most accurately by a person who sees it break through the mist at unexpected moments—a person who experiences sudden clear images. A writer, being conscientious, is always straining his eyes for this moment, peering ahead and around; consequently when the moment of revelation comes, his eyes are poppy and tired and his sensitized mind has become fogged by the too-frequent half-stimuli of imagined sight. No figure is more pitiful to contemplate than a novelist with a thousand-dollar advance from a publishing house and a date when the manuscript is due. He knows he must invite his soul, but he is compelled to add: "And don't be late, soul!"

HONOR ROLL

1/11/30

THE *Nation* HAS PUT *The New Yorker* on its Honor Roll for 1929, along with Rear Admiral Byrd, the New York *Telegram,* Professor Michelson, Eva Le Gallienne, and the United States Senate. Here are the very words of the announcement: "The *New Yorker,* for being consistently amusing, good-tempered, intelligent, resourceful, and good-to-look-at." We are naturally grateful; it is the first time anybody has put us on an honor list. But after thus elevating us, the *Nation,* in an explanatory paragraph, plunges us into despair. "We had great trouble," said they, "in deciding whether to give first place, on the score of humor, to the *New Yorker* or to the Department of State. We finally gave it to the *New Yorker* on the ground that our cheerful contemporary is always good-natured, which the State Department sometimes is not. But we confess that we find the State Department a great deal funnier than the *New Yorker.*" To us this comparison seems unfair. No magazine, whether weekly or annual, could ever hope to be as funny as the State Department. We defy most magazines to be as funny, even, as the Passport Bureau. In a comedic moment of history such as today, with its funny taxes, its funny prohibition, its funny prosperity, and its funny talk of peace, a mere publication whose aim is to interpret the times is somewhat at a loss to compete, in entertaining qualities, with the institutions themselves. We often feel like giving up and going home.

UNWRITTEN

4/26/30

SOMETIMES WE REGRET OUR FAILURE to write about things that really interest us. The reason we fail is probably that to write about them would prove embarrassing. The things that interested us during the past week, for example, and that we were unable or unwilling to write about (things that stand out clear as pictures in our head) were: the look in the eye of a man whose overcoat, with velvet collar, was held together by a bit of string; the appearance of an office after the building had shut down for the night, and the obvious futility of the litter; the head and shoulders of a woman in a lighted window, combing her hair with infinite care, making it smooth and neat so that it would attract someone who would want to muss it up; Osgood Perkins in love with Lillian Gish; a man on a bicycle on Fifth Avenue; a short eulogy of John James Audubon, who spent his life loafing around, painting birds; an entry in Art Young's diary, about a sick farmer who didn't know what was the matter with himself but thought it was probably biliousness; and the sudden impulse that we had (and very nearly gratified) to upend a large desk for the satisfaction of seeing everything on it slide off slowly onto the floor.

ACCELERATING CULTURE

5/21/38

A CALL HAS GONE OUT TO WRITERS to meet on Sunday in the cause of a Federal Bureau of Fine Arts. "In issuing this call," said the letter we received, "we are moved by a belief that it is the desire of all writers . . . to have the advance of culture accelerated, the base of art broadened, and the economic place of artists reasonably secure."

Here, in a sentence, is the issue. One must decide how he feels about the acceleration of culture before he can know whether he wants a Bureau of Fine Arts. It is as common to believe that culture should be accelerated as to believe that whooping cough should be retarded, yet we have never heard any devotee of the bureaucratic ideal make out a solid case for this proposed quickening. A Bureau of Fine Arts would indeed accelerate culture, in that it would provide public money for creative enterprise, and by so doing would make it easier for artists and writers to go on being artists and writers, as well as for persons who are not artists and writers to continue the happy pretence. Such a Bureau would presumably have other effects symptomatic of acceleration. The radio, for example, has immensely accelerated culture in that it has brought to millions of people, in torrential measure, the distant and often adulterated sounds of art and life. But it is still an open question whether this mysterious electrical diffusion has been a blessing to man, who appears at the moment to be most unhappy about nearly everything.

Santayana, although he won't be at the meeting Sunday, is a writer whose views on the diffusion of culture we find instructive. "Great thoughts," he says, "require a great mind and pure beauties a profound sensibility. To attempt to give such things a wide currency is to be willing to denaturalize them in order to boast that they have been propagated. Culture is on the horns of this dilemma: if profound and noble it must remain rare, if common it must become mean. These alternatives can never be eluded until some purified and high-bred race succeeds the promiscuous bipeds that now blacken the planet."

Advocates of a bureaucratic culture, in wishing to establish artists more firmly in the national economy, argue that it is to a nation's advantage to make its creative souls more comfortable financially; but here we feel they are confusing an aesthetic ideal with a social one. When two persons are in need of food, there is always the embarrassing question whether to feed the talented one first, on the somewhat questionable grounds that he may live to provide beauty for the other one (who in the meanwhile may die of starvation, or laughter). This is essentially what the Bureau proposes, and it is a proposal which naturally meets with very little opposition among writers and artists, who feel both hunger and beauty, and who can always use a little dough.

Sponsorship of the creative ideal by the government has many delightful delinquencies. It assumes, among other things, that art is recognizable in embryo—or at least recognizable enough to make it worth the public's while to pay for raising the baby. And it assumes that artists, like chickens, are responsive to proper diet. We sometimes wonder if they are. Housman, when they asked him what caused him to produce poems, said that as far as he could determine it was usually some rather inappropriate physical disability, such as a relaxed sore throat. This catarrhal theory of the creative life has always fascinated us, and it should give the government pause before setting aside too great a share of the public funds for improving the vigor of poets.

OUR CONTENTIOUS READERS

4/6/40

TO THE EDITOR OF *The New Yorker*,

Dear Sir:

Students of City College are almost certain to be misled by Bishop Manning's attack on Bertrand Russell.* They will conclude that the issue is a moral one, and that Earl Russell's sex ideas must be accepted or rejected on the score of morality. This is most unfortunate. The trouble with Russell on sex is not that he is immoral but that he is unrealistic. He is just a dreamer, putting into logical expression the immoderate hopes of men for a more elastic, carefree, and generally agreeable solution of their urgencies and their problems. College students are quick to explore any ethical concept which has the double bloom of intellectuality and sin; I think the Bishop was most unwise to invest the Russell ethics with the glamour of wickedness and to advertise the Russell code as "immoral," thereby giving it a distinction it hardly deserves. Students will certainly infer that if Russell's sex ideas are as bad as all that, there must be something to them; whereas the depressing thing about Earl Russell's code is that it doesn't work. However distinguished he may be in the world of logical thought, on the subject of sex he has always been something of an old fraud.

Let us consider two or three of the sex concepts which the Bishop dug up in his investigation. First, he quotes from Russell's "Education and the Modern World":

> I am sure that university life would be better, both
> intellectually and morally, if most university students had
> temporary childless marriages. This would afford a solution of
> the sexual urge neither restless nor surreptitious, neither
> mercenary nor casual, and of such a nature that it need not
> take up time which ought to be given to work.

*British philosopher and mathematician (3rd Earl Russell). His appointment as professor of philosophy at City College of New York was rescinded when Jean Kay, a taxpayer protesting his appointment, brought suit in New York's State Supreme Court against the Board of Higher Education and Justice John E. McGeehan ruled in her favor. Spearheading the opposition to Russell, William T. Manning, the Episcopal Bishop of New York, had sent a circular letter to the New York newspapers denouncing Russell's appointment. The case created public debate not only over Russell, but also over issues of academic freedom.

Now, the suggestion that to live with a girl isn't going to take up much of a student's time seems to me as fantastic a bit of philosophical hokum as I have ever encountered. Russell is a Britisher, and of course I don't know how things are in England, but I think I am safe in saying that in America nothing takes up more of a man's time than living with a girl. It is the most time-consuming thing there is. Also, I resent the implication in this passage of Russell's that sex is just something to get out of your system, that work is the important thing, and that sex is good just in proportion to the amount of a man's time it *doesn't* occupy. That's a mighty unattractive report to spread among the young, who are (rightly, I think) romantically minded, and who tend to incorporate sex into the body of the romance.

Then we come to the Earl's remark that "if a man and woman choose to live together, that should be nobody's business but their own." If the Bishop were smart, he would simply point out to students that the word to watch out for in that sentence is the word "should." Of course it *should* be nobody's business but their own. But it usually turns out to be the business of the darnedest, most unexpected people, including a young man in the same building who has been secretly in love with the girl for three years, has sublimated his passion by tearing telephone books in two, and now seizes the opportunity to hang himself with a rope made out of dozens of college pennants. Students should certainly be informed that no man, since the beginning of time, has lived with a woman without it turning out sooner or later to be somebody else's business.

Finally, there is the Earl's little essay on the psychology of adultery. "Suppose," writes Earl Russell eagerly, "a man has to be away from home on business for a number of months. If he is physically vigorous, he will find it difficult to remain continent throughout this time, however fond he may be of his wife." I think Bishop Manning should just tell the students that the matter of continence during a business trip has very little to do with physical vigor. An exceptionally vigorous man almost invariably spends himself in rather forthright, athletic ways—leaping up stairs three steps at a time, pounding on other men's desks, and putting in long-distance calls from clients' offices. It is the tired little fellow on his way home from a basal-metabolism test who is most likely to become hopelessly involved in some adulterous and unhappy circumstance quite beyond his puny control. In my professional life (I am a doctor), I have enjoyed the confidence of hundreds of adulterous persons; rarely have they shown evidences of any special vigor. As a group, they are on the anemic side.

These are only a few of the points which the Bishop has been worried about. I merely wished to suggest to him that if he wants to spike Russell's guns, he is going about it the hard way.

Yours faithfully,
WALTER TITHRIDGE, M.D.*

EDITORIAL WRITERS

3/4/44

GEORGE SELDES, in the *Saturday Review*, says he has never known of an editorial writer who wrote as he pleased. This makes us a kept man. We often wonder about our life in our bordello, whether such an existence erodes one's character or builds it. An editorial page is a fuzzy performance, any way you look at it, since it affects a composite personality with an editorial "we" for a front. Once in a while we think of ourself as "we," but not often. The word "ourself" is the giveaway—the plural "our," the singular "self," united in a common cause. "Ourself" is real. It means "over-self," which reminds us that we should try to dig up a writer named Emerson for this page.

At any rate, we have evolved (and this may interest Mr. Seldes) a system for the smooth operation of a literary bordello. The system is this: We write as we please, and the magazine publishes as *it* pleases. When the two pleasures coincide, something gets into print. When they don't, the reader draws a blank. It is a system we recommend—the only one, in fact,

*A pseudonym used by White.

under which we are willing to be kept. Mr. Seldes can undoubtedly prove that it comes to the same, in the end, as if we deliberately shaped our ideas to a prescribed pattern, but in order to do that he will have to write another article, so at least we've made work for somebody and are not entirely frivolous and useless. Of course, a good deal depends on the aims of a publication. The more devious the motives of his employer, the more difficult for a writer to write as he pleases. As far as we have been able to discover, the keepers of this house have two aims: the first is to make money, the second is to make sense. We have watched for other motives, but we have never turned up any. That makes for good working conditions, and we write this as a sort of small, delayed tribute to our house. Anytime Mr. Seldes wants to see writers writing as they please, he can just step off the elevator and take a gander at us. By us, of course, we mean ourself. Emerson's the name. Call us Ralph.

RAINBOW WORKERS

11/1/47

THIS MAGAZINE TRAFFICS with all sorts of questionable characters, some of them, no doubt, infiltrating. Our procedure so far has been to examine the manuscript, not the writer; the picture, not the artist. We have not required a statement of political belief or a blood count. This still seems like a sensible approach to the publishing problem, although falling short of Representative J. Parnell Thomas's* standard. One thing we

*Chairman of the House Un-American Activities Committee. This committee, set up as a standing committee of the House of Representatives in 1945, investigated charges of Communist influences in government and other areas of American life (such as the motion picture industry). White, as a teenager, once took Thomas's sister Eileen to a tea dance; for an account of that date see "Afternoon of an American Boy" in *Essays of E. B. White.*

have always enjoyed about our organization is the splashy, rainbow effect of the workers: Red blending into Orange, Orange
blending into Yellow, and so on, right across the spectrum to
Violet. (Hi, Violet!) We sit among as quietly seething a mass of
reactionaries, revolutionaries, worn-out robber barons, tawny
pipits, liberals, Marxists in funny hats, and Taftists in pin stripes
as ever gathered under one roof in a common enterprise. The
group seems healthy enough, in a messy sort of way, and everybody finally meets everybody else at the water cooler, like
beasts at the water hole in the jungle. There is one man here
who believes that the solution to everything is proper mulching—the deep mulch. Russia to him is just another mulch problem. We have them all. Our creative activity, whether un- or
non-un-American, is properly not on a loyalty basis but merely
on a literacy basis—a dreamy concept. If this should change,
and we should go over to loyalty, the meaning of "un-American
activity" would change, too, since the America designated in
the phrase would not be the same country we have long lived
in and admired.

We ran smack into the loyalty question the other day when
we got a phone call from another magazine, asking us what we
knew about a man they had just hired. He was a man whose
pieces we had published, from time to time, and they wanted
to know about him. "What's his political slant?" our inquisitor
asked. We replied that we didn't have any idea, and that the
matter had never come up. This surprised our questioner
greatly, but not as much as his phone call surprised us. When
he hung up, we dialled Weather and listened to the rising wind.

EXPEDIENCY

1/31/48

WE HAVE OFTEN WONDERED how journalism schools go about preparing young men and women for newspaperdom and magazineland. An answer came just the other day, in a surprising form. It came from California, via *Editor & Publisher.* We quote:

> San Francisco—Public opinion polls are scientific tools which should be used by newspapers to prevent editorial errors of judgment, Dr. Chilton Bush, head of the Division of Journalism at Stanford University, believes.
>
> "A publisher is smart to take a poll before he gets his neck out too far," he said. "Polls provide a better idea of acceptance of newspaper policies."

We have read this statement half a dozen times, probably in the faint hope that *Editor & Publisher* might be misquoting Dr. Bush or that we had failed to understand him. But there it stands—a clear guide to the life of expediency, a simple formula for journalism by acceptance, a short essay on how to run a newspaper by saying only the words the public wants to hear said. It seems to us that Dr. Bush hands his students not a sword but a weather vane. Under such conditions, the fourth estate becomes a mere parody of the human intelligence, and had best be turned over to bright birds with split tongues or to monkeys who can make change.

ACCREDITED WRITERS?

12/11/48

BEFORE A BOOK CAN BE PUBLISHED in Czechoslovakia, the publisher must submit an outline of it to the government for approval. Accompanying the outline must be written opinions of "responsible literary critics, scientists, or writers." (We are quoting from a dispatch to the *Times*.) The question of who is a responsible critic or writer comes up in every country, of course. It must have come up here when the Algonquin Hotel advertised special weekend rates for "accredited writers." We often used to wonder just how the Algonquin arrived at the answer to the fascinating question of who is an accredited writer, and whether the desk clerk required of an applicant a rough draft of an impending novel. It seems to us that the Czech government is going to be in a spot, too. No true critic or writer is "responsible" in the political sense which this smelly edict implies, and in order to get the kind of censorship the government obviously wants, the government will need to go a step further and require that the critic himself be certified by a responsible party, and then a step beyond that and require that the responsible party be vouched for. This leads to infinity, and to no books. Which is probably the goal of the Czech government.

The matter of who is, and who isn't, a responsible writer or scientist reminds us of the famous phrase in Marxist doctrine— the phrase that is often quoted and that has won many people to Communism as a theory of life: "From each according to his ability; to each according to his needs." Even after you have contemplated the sheer beauty of this concept, you are left holding the sheer problem of accreditation: who is needy, who is able? Again the desk clerk looms—a shadowy man. And behind the clerk another clerk, for an accreditation checkup. And so it goes. Who shall be the man who has the authority to establish our innermost need, who shall be the one to approve the standard of achievement of which we are capable? Perhaps, as democracy assumes, every man is a writer, every man wholly needy, every man capable of unimaginable deeds. It isn't as beautiful to the ear as the Marxian phrase, maybe, but there's an idea there somewhere.

SATIRE ON DEMAND

1/8/49

ONE OF OUR CONTEMPORARIES, the Russian humor magazine called *Crocodile,* has been under fire lately. *Crocodile* got word from Higher Up that it would have to improve, would have to bear down harder on "the vestiges of capitalism in the consciousness of the people." This directive, according to the Associated Press, came straight from the Central Committee and was unusual only for its admission that there were any such vestiges. *Crocodile* was instructed to gird on its satiric pen and by "the weapons of satire to expose the thieves of public property, grafters, bureaucrats . . ." It has never been our good fortune to observe a controlled-press satirist who is under instructions from his government to get funnier, but it is a sight we'd gladly crawl under a curtain to see. A person really flowers as a satirist when he first slips *out* of control, and a working satirist (of whom there are woefully few in any country) careens as wildly as a car with no brakes. To turn out an acceptable pasquinade is probably unthinkable under controlled conditions, for the spirit of satire is the spirit of independence. Apparently the Russian committee anticipates difficulties in stepping up humor and satire by decree. *Crocodile* used to be a weekly. From now on it will appear only every ten days. Three extra days each issue, for straining.

THE THUD OF IDEAS

9/23/50

AMERICANS ARE WILLING to go to enormous trouble and expense defending their principles with arms, very little trouble and expense advocating them with words. Temperamentally we are ready to die for certain principles (or, in the case of overripe adults, send youngsters to die), but we show little inclination to advertise the reasons for the dying. Some critics say that a self-governing, democratic people don't know what they believe; but that is nonsense. It is simply that a democratic people, who are also an impatient and restless people, feel no strong urge to define what they instinctively comprehend. Also, they do not delegate to government the power to speak for the individual. The disinclination to propagandize is characteristic. Thirty-six billions for a military program, a thin buck for a voice clarifying our aims and beliefs. Many people now think, and we agree with them, that if we are to compete successfully with the throaty call of the Communist heartland—a call as brassy as that of a tenting evangelist—we shall have to develop a bit of a whistle of our own. We already have the Soviet voice at a disadvantage, and we should exploit it. The Russians limit themselves to spreading what they call the Truth and to jamming the sounds that come from the other direction. They cannot disseminate information, because information would too often embarrass their Truth. We can do much better. We can, and should, spread the material an American reads each morning in his paper—news, definitions, letters to the editor, texts, credos, reports, recipes, aims and intentions. We must reach and astonish with our kind of reporting the millions who hear almost nothing of that sort and who hardly know it exists. We can safely leave Truth to the Kremlin, and can broadcast instead the splendid fact of difference of opinion, the thud of ideas in collision.

The Russian charge about us, which deliberately misleads so many millions of people, should be met by a greatly expanded United States Department of Correction, Amplification, and Abuse. Misinformation, even when it is not deliberate, is at the bottom of much human misery. We recall the recent ordeal of

33

George Kuscinkas, the fifty-six-year-old delivery man who pushed his handcart thirteen miles, far into the Bronx, because his employer had written "23rd Street" so that it looked like "234th Street." This was mere carelessness. But think of the journeys that are being made in the world by those who are pushing a heavy handcart in an impossible direction under misapprehensions of one sort and another!

We saw a piece in the paper the other day by a historian who had decided that freedom was shot because frontiers were disappearing. Freedom, he reasoned, can't survive in the congested conditions of a non-pioneering civilization. If there were anything to this theory, it would be the worst news of the week. We think the historian underestimates the vitality of the free spirit in the individual and exaggerates the role of geography. An iron curtain almost but not quite impenetrable is as challenging a frontier as a forest of virgin timber. Besides, it is perfectly apparent that freedom resides comfortably in areas of great congestion. We walked through such a street this morning.

Somehow the letters-to-the-editor page, strange and wonderful as it always is, is one of the chief adornments of the society we love and seek to clarify for the world. The privilege of writing to the editor is basic; the product is the hot dish of scrambled eggs that is America. Take the *Times* the other morning: a resounding letter headed "Awareness of Issues Asked," a studious appeal to protect forest preserves ("Let this long and difficult fight be a lesson . . ."), an indignant attack by a Gaines Dog Research man on the superstition that dog days are associated with hydrophobia, a thoughtful essay on world government, and finally a blast from a reader in Monroe, New York: "It just so happens that I attempted to transplant three plants [of orange milkweed] recently and they all had long, horizontal roots."

Such a page, together with the *Times*' sense of duty in publishing it, suggests an abiding normalcy in democratic behavior and thought, and gives the reassurance that neither Korea nor the volume of the Russian voice can unsettle this land whose citizens' torments and hopes, big and little, are aired daily in the press, this land whose roots are both long and horizontal.

THE HUMOR PARADOX

9/27/52

ADLAI STEVENSON* has been reprimanded by General Eisenhower for indulging in humor and wit, and Mr. Stevenson
has very properly been warned of the consequences by his own
party leaders, who are worried. Their fears are well grounded.
We have had long experience with humor in the literary world,
and we add our warning to the other warnings. Nothing is so
suspect as humor, nothing so surely brands a work of art or
politics as second-rate. It has been our sad duty on several
occasions in the past to issue admonitory statements concerning the familiar American paradox that governs humor: every
American, to the last man, lays claim to a "sense" of humor and
guards it as his most significant spiritual trait, yet rejects humor
as a contaminating element wherever found. America is a nation of comics and comedians; nevertheless, humor has no stature and is accepted only after the death of the perpetrator.
Almost the only first-string American statesman who managed
to combine high office with humor was Lincoln, and he was
murdered finally. Churchill is, in our opinion, a man of humor,
but he lives in England, where it doesn't count.

The New Yorker subscribes to a press-clipping bureau, and
over the years we have examined thousands of clippings from
many sources, in praise of one thing or another that has appeared in the magazine. Almost invariably, the praise begins
with a qualifying remark, pointing out that the magazine is
non-serious in nature and indicating that it takes a superior
intelligence (the writer's) to detect truth or merit in such unlikely surroundings. If it's any comfort to Stevenson, we can
assure him that in this matter of humor we have been in the
same boat with him for a long time, and that the sea has been
rough.

*Stevenson was the Democratic nominee for President in 1952, Dwight Eisen-
hower the Republican nominee.

AFFAIR WITH HUMOR

10/5/46

SOMEBODY, perhaps suspecting that we were having an affair with Humor, sent us the following passage from Proudhon. We reprint it in free translation, with pride and embarrassment—the sort of mixed feeling you have when walking with a pretty girl and the girl is whistled at:

> Liberty, like Reason, does not exist or manifest itself except by the constant disdain of its own works; it perishes as soon as it is filled with self-approval. That is why humor has always been a characteristic of philosophical and liberal genius, the seal of the human spirit, the irresistible instrument of progress. Stagnant peoples are always solemn peoples: the man of a people that laughs is a thousand times closer to reason and liberty than the anchorite who prays or the philosopher who argues.
>
> Humor—true liberty!—it is you who deliver me from ambition for power, from servitude to party, from respect for routine, from the pedantry of science, from admiration for celebrities, from the mystifications of politics, from the fanaticism of the reformers, from fear of this great universe, and from self-admiration.
>
> Come, sovereign, turn a ray of your light on my fellow-citizens; kindle in their soul a spark of your spirit, so that my confession may reconcile them to each other and so that this inevitable revolution may come about with serenity and joy.

Proudhon's word is *"l'ironie,"* which we have translated "humor," possibly too loosely, but at any rate with serenity and joy. After so many summers and winters living with Humor as our mistress and credit manager, seeing her blow hot and cold, running her unreasonable errands, taking her lip, we find our affection undiminished. The attachment strengthens, even as it grows more troublesome. Come, sovereign, give us a kiss. And deliver us, right this minute, from self-admiration.

3

Thoreau

THE INDIVIDUALIST

5/7/49

MAY 6TH IS THE SADDEST DAY in the year for us, as it is the day of Thoreau's death*—a grief from which we have not recovered. Henry Thoreau has probably been more wildly misconstrued than any other person of comparable literary stature. He got a reputation for being a naturalist, and he was not much of a naturalist. He got a reputation for being a hermit, and he was no hermit. He was a writer, is what he was. Many regarded him as a poseur. He was a poseur, all right, but the pose was struck not for other people to study but for *him* to study—a brave and ingenious device for a creative person to adopt. He posed for himself and was both artist and model, examining his own position in relation to nature and society with the most patient and appreciative care. "Walden" is so indigestible that many hungry people abandon it because it makes them mildly sick, each sentence being an anchovy spread, and the whole thing too salty and nourishing for one sitting. Henry was torn all his days between two awful pulls—the gnawing desire to change life, and the equally troublesome desire to live it. This is the explanation of his excursion. He hated Negro slavery and helped slaves escape, but he hated even more the self-imposed bondage of men who hung chains about their necks simply because it was the traditional way to live. Because of a few crotchety remarks he made about the factory system and because of his essay on civil disobedience, he is one of the early Americans now being taken up by Marx-

*White admired Henry David Thoreau, author of *Walden*, perhaps more than he did any other writer. In the following pieces and in "A Slight Sound at Evening" *(Essays)*, "Walden" *(One Man's Meat)*, and "The Retort Transcendental" *(Second Tree)*, White records his appreciation for *Walden:* "the book is like an invitation to life's dance."

ists. But not even these hard-working Johnnies-come-lately can pin him down; he subscribed to no economic system and his convictions were strong but disorderly. What seemed so wrong to him was less man's economy than man's puny spirit and man's strained relationship with nature—which he regarded as a public scandal. Most of the time he didn't want to do anything about anything—he wanted to observe and to feel. "What demon possessed me that I behaved so well?" he wrote—a sentence that is 100-proof anchovy. And when he died he uttered the purest religious thought we ever heard. They asked him whether he had made his peace with God and he replied, "I was not aware we had quarrelled." He was the subtlest humorist of the nineteenth century, a most religious man, and was awake every moment. He never slept, except in bed at night.

WALDEN

12/28/46

THE MOST RECENT EDITION of "Walden" is a Dodd, Mead book containing a hundred and forty-two photographs by Edwin Way Teale. It is an amusing specimen for hard-shelled Thoreauvians. In it they can hear one naturalist speaking to another across a hundred years. Mr. Teale supplies, in addition to the pictures, an excellent introduction and some background notes for each chapter. Carrying a camera, and probably bent on elevating his life by a conscious endeavor, he went out to the pond to make a photographic record of where Thoreau lived and of what he lived for. Mr. Teale rose early to catch the mists above the water. He lay in wait for the ice to break up in spring. He went out and took pictures of Brister's Spring and of Fair Haven Hill. He walked the tracks of the Fitchburg. He closed in on ground nut and swamp grass, on johnswort and wild grape. He even fired point-blank at a bean row and scored a direct hit.

"Walden" is, of course, not a book that can be illustrated. The Concord woods are both tamer and wilder than they were in 1845, and besides, Thoreau was writing not about beans but about the meaning of beans—which is hard to photograph. A person who is about to encounter the text of "Walden" for the first time should buy a small, unadorned edition, such as the pocket Oxford, which will allow him to travel light and on a high plane. I rather imagine that Henry Thoreau would feel that Mr. Teale, roaming the Concord woods on his second-hand errand, was not fronting the essential facts, not living deliberately. Nevertheless, it is easy to understand why Mr. Teale was there, easy to share his vicarious excitement and to enjoy his tardy and beautiful photographs. (I was glad to learn from one of the notes that Thoreau was thirty-six years old before he discovered that he was tying his shoes with a granny knot. A man must take courage from something these days, while tying his shoes, and that is as buoyant a thought as any.)

A book of this sort is a personal tribute rather than an illustrative work. Thoreau is the naturalist's philosopher. The extraordinary thing about him was that he so strangely combined the curiosity, the patience, and the literalness of the scientist with the poetical and critical faculty of the artist. His contribution to limnology (the study of fresh-water ponds) is recognized by scientists. And even when he was voicing man's highest aspirations in sentences of great power and intensity, a muskrat would somehow work its way into the thing. As long as there are men and muskrats, there will be readers who will ache to identify themselves with the spirit and the sense of this revolutionary book, this solid and everlasting book; and they will be drawn to Deep Cove in all weather and in all seasons, armed with whatever they can substitute for a borrowed axe. Teale took a camera.

THOREAU AND SHELTER

8/7/48

THE THOREAU SOCIETY wants contributions so it can buy the house at 73 Main Street, Concord, where Henry David Thoreau sat taking pot shots at the whole theory of shelter. We haven't decided yet whether to listen to the Society or to Henry. If we heed the Society's call, it will cost us a hundred dollars to become a one-three-hundredths owner of 73 Main, but if we take Thoreau's advice, we'll simply enclose a dollar to the Society and suggest that it exercise a little Yankee shrewdness and buy one of those large toolboxes that you see by the railroad, six feet long and three feet wide, bore a few auger holes in it, and set it up in Concord, thus memorializing not only the man but the Idea. Unless the Thoreau Society is careful, it is going to find itself with a museum on its hands—a labyrinth without a clue. Nobody would chuckle more appreciatively over this, if he were in chuckling trim, than Henry. You can hear his frogs chuckling over it any night you want to walk out to the pond.

VISITORS TO THE POND

WHEN SENATOR MCCARTHY* turned his attention to H. D. Thoreau, the egghead of Concord, and decided to visit the Walden country to look into the very suspicious fact of Thoreau's pondside interlude, he asked me to go along as guide. I always jump at the chance of an outing and I agreed readily. Copies of "Walden, or Life in the Woods" had been found on the shelves of libraries of the United States Information Service overseas, and the Senator was in a high state of excitement about it. He was particularly anxious that I accompany him to the pond, as he wanted me to read aloud from the pocket edition, which has fine print. Long hours of studying defamatory evidence have affected McCarthy's vision, and there are days when he can hardly see anything smaller than a subpoena.

The minute we stepped from the train at the Concord station, the indescribable innocence and beneficence of Nature began having a bad effect on my companion. It was a lovely afternoon, and I suggested that we walk out to the pond along the tracks of the Fitchburg Railroad, but McCarthy refused irritably and demanded a cab.

"I'd like to walk," I protested.

"And I want to ride," snapped the Senator. It was a contretemps.

"A contretemps!" cried a bystander, and several other Concordians, idling on the platform, gathered around to see the fun.

Seizing the opportunity, I pulled "Walden" from my pocket and turned quickly to page 119, knowing that I could use the text to mollify the Senator. "Here," I said. "We'll let Thoreau himself settle the point whether we walk or ride. Here's the passage: 'I have found that no exertion of the legs can bring two minds much nearer to one another.'"

"There you are!" said the Senator. "We ride."

*Joseph McCarthy, chairman of the Senate's Government Operations Committee. McCarthy held publicized hearings accusing people of sympathizing with the Communist Party. He was censured in 1954 by Senate colleagues. White frequently spoke out against McCarthy and his tactics.

As I climbed into the cab behind my strong-willed companion, I could see that his spirits were mounting because of the little incident that I had so deftly turned in his favor. At the pond, we paid off the driver and I led the Senator rapidly along the path, showing him Deep Cove and the site of the cabin. McCarthy cased the woodland quickly. He explained that he liked to "get the feel" of a person's background before going after him. As we were standing there, imbibing the past through every pore, a skunk appeared on the path, eyed us curiously, turned, and walked away. The Senator chuckled.

"What's funny, Senator?" I inquired.

"Young man," he replied (he kept calling me "young man," although I am ten years his senior), "young man, one thing you'll find out—everywhere you go in this country you'll come across a skunk." The episode seemed to please him immensely and his mood was now mellow. He was soon grilling me closely about Thoreau's character, habits, and associates.

"How big was the house?" he asked.

"Ten by fifteen," I replied.

"How big was the mortgage?"

"There wasn't any," I said, weakly. The Senator's eyes narrowed. He drew a notebook and pencil from his pocket and scribbled, "Says there was no mortgage."

"I consider it un-American not to have a mortgage," murmured the Senator, as though speaking to himself. "Besides, it's probably a lie."

"Well, this case was a little different," I explained. "The whole house cost only a little over twenty-eight dollars. That was for materials. Thoreau did the work himself."

"I'd certainly like to see a breakdown of *those* figures," muttered the Senator. So I showed him page 42 and read him the modest accounting.

Suddenly McCarthy turned on me. "Answer a simple question!" he said. "Did this man believe in the American way of life?"

"I will answer that," I replied, "if you will tell me what you mean by the American way of life."

A foxy smile spread across the Senator's face as he detected the trap I had laid for him. "Young man," he said, "I praise Americanism, I don't define it. If you define it, you lose customers. But let's get down to business. Let's get to the book!"

I was more than willing. "Walden" is the only book I own,

although there are some others unclaimed on my shelves. Every man, I think, reads one book in his life, and this one is mine. It is not the best book I ever encountered, perhaps, but it is for me the handiest, and I keep it about me in much the same way one carries a handkerchief—for relief in moments of defluxion or despair. So I was glad to get to the book at this juncture. The Senator sat down on the ground and propped himself against a log, and I joined him after kicking an empty beer can out of the way.

"Read from the chapter on Economy and from the chapter on Solitude!" commanded the Senator. "Every screwball who tries to discuss economics gives himself away, and as for solitude, that's damaging in itself. It's un-American to live alone."

Slipping the book from my pocket, I opened it to the first page and started to read, at first hesitantly, then gaining confidence.

" 'When I wrote the following pages, or rather the bulk of them, I lived alone, in the woods, a mile from any neighbor, in a house which I had built myself, on the shore of Walden Pond, in Concord, Massachusetts, and earned my living by the labor of my hands only. I lived there two years and two months. At present I am a sojourner in civilized life again.' "

The familiar words had a new, strange sound—a sort of looseness, as though they were sifting down through the branches of the pines and skittering up from the surface of the lake. The Senator attended closely. He was obviously a good listener.

" 'I should not obtrude my affairs so much on the notice of my readers if very particular inquiries had not been made by my townsmen concerning my mode of life, which some would call impertinent . . .' "

McCarthy leapt to his feet. "Inquiries?" he snorted. "There you are. This guy was being investigated even then, and the inquiries were being called impertinent. Brother, where have I heard *that* before! Anyway, the townspeople must have been wise to him or they wouldn't have questioned his affairs."

The Senator took out his pad and noted, "Was under fire at the time." Then he ordered me to continue reading. I complied, skipping around in the text as it suited my fancy, which is one of the privileges of anyone who reads to the blind or the near-blind.

" 'The greater part of what my neighbors call good I believe in my soul to be bad . . .' "

"Read that again, slower!" commanded the Senator.

I repeated the sentence.

"Well," drawled McCarthy, "that's a subversive statement right there. He's going against the majority opinion of the community. Anybody who does that has no kick coming if he gets investigated." The Senator grew thoughtful. He repeated the sentence slowly, savoring the words. "You know," he said, "that sentence came very near being a very sensible remark. I could edit it a little and make it into something completely American, if I wanted to. All you do is just take out three words. Listen to this: 'The greater part of my neighbors I believe in my soul to be bad.' Now you've got something! Well, I'm not going to clean up Thoreau's text for him—he's cutting his own throat fast and I'm going to let him. But it just shows what can be done if you're on the ball. Read some more!"

" 'I think we may safely trust a good deal more than we do,' " I read.

"Poppycock!" cried McCarthy. "Balderdash!" He was visibly shaken by the sound of the word "trust," and his body was racked with shudders. He flapped his head back and forth, the way a dog fights an itch, as though trying to expunge the idea of confidence from his thoughts. I waited till he subsided, then skipped a few paragraphs and read some of Thoreau's remarks about shelter and vital heat.

" 'When a man is warmed by the several modes which I have described, what does he want next? Surely not more warmth of the same kind, as more and richer food, larger and more splendid houses, finer and more abundant clothing . . .' "

"Wait a minute!" said the Senator. "Now d'ya see what I mean? This man was Communist-inspired. That accounts for his sour attitude about housing—those cracks about not wanting larger and more splendid houses, more food, finer clothing. Every good American wants a bigger house, that's for sure."

"What about the small ranch-type dwelling so popular today?" I asked, timidly. "The ranch-type house is an American manifestation, a concession to the compact-living school of which Thoreau was a founder. Thoreau was simply ahead of his time."

McCarthy uttered something unintelligible. He seemed unimpressed. I was unimpressed myself, but I felt that I had met the challenge adroitly and in a manly fashion. I turned back to the book, but my companion interrupted.

"Was this fellow ever in jail?"

"Yes," I replied.

"I thought so," said the Senator. "Why was he in?"

"Nonpayment of taxes," I said. This cheered the Senator and we were able to return to the text.

" 'For many years I was self-appointed inspector of snow-storms and rain-storms, and did my duty faithfully; surveyor, if not of highways, then of forest paths and all across-lots routes, keeping them open, and ravines bridged and passable at all seasons, where the public heel had testified to their utility.' "

" 'The public heel?' " repeated the Senator. "The Acheson* of his day, I reckon." I responded to the weak joke and we laughed together. A loon on the far side of the pond heard us and laughed back, mocking us across the water. McCarthy's face clouded at the unearthly sound. A look of anger furrowed his brow. "Nobody mocks McCarthy!" he growled. He shook his fist angrily at the bird, and tension mounted darkly in the woods. I hastily retreated to the text, wondering vaguely how this strange excursion of ours was helping the United States Information Service, which now seemed incredibly remote.

" 'I have thought that Walden Pond would be a good place for business,' " I read, " 'not solely on account of the railroad and the ice trade; it offers advantages which it may not be good policy to divulge; it is a good port and a good foundation. No Neva marshes to be filled; though you must everywhere build on piles of your own driving. It is said that a flood-tide, with a westerly wind, and ice in the Neva, would sweep St. Petersburg from the face of the earth.' "

"That does it," said McCarthy, quietly. "He's hung himself right there in a single paragraph. First he admits that his lonely hangout has advantages he's unwilling to divulge, then he bewails the loss of a Russian city. What more do I want? I can get the book yanked from overseas libraries on that one paragraph alone. The taxpayers won't have to foot the bill any longer for this kind of fruitcake. The lousy jailbird!"

---

*Dean Acheson, Secretary of State 1949–53. Although he helped create the Cold War policies of containment of communism ("negotiation through strength"), he was attacked during the McCarthy hearings for refusing to fire any of his State Department subordinates. "I will not turn my back on Alger Hiss," he said.

"Not so fast, Senator!" I put in, and rose to my full height. "When you cast aspersions on Henry David Thoreau you are impeaching a great American institution."

"What institution?"

"The motel," I replied with quiet desperation. "It is well known that the man who conceived the motel got his inspiration from Thoreau's pondside hut. In fact, you might say that the tiny Walden house was America's first motel."

I was grasping at a straw. Actually, I found myself grasping at the stalk of a smooth sumac *(Rhus glabra);* it gave way and I swayed into the bushes, fell, and buried my teeth in leafmold. McCarthy smelled a ruse and didn't even dignify my motel story with a reply. "Skip the rest of Economy," he ordered, "and get on to Solitude! On second thought, skip Solitude, too. I've had enough of this bilge. We'll go back to town."

"Along the railroad tracks?" I pleaded, sitting up and spitting leafmold.

"Along Route 126," replied the Senator. He had his way, as usual, and we trudged wearily into Concord along the highway and put up at the Inn, where we spent a restless night in a double room.

On the plane carrying us back next morning—I to New York, McCarthy to Washington—the Senator was in a thoughtful mood. He kept steering the conversation back to Thoreau.

"Frankly, what would you say was eating the guy up?" he asked. "Just what *was* on his mind?"

"A fair question," I said, stalling. "Let's see, now—what was on Henry's mind? Goodness! What *wasn't?* Well, for one thing, he was on the defensive; he felt at home in nature as well as in society, and to that extent was freakish. He had a good opinion of wildness. He liked to test ideas on his tongue before swallowing them, and was more than half convinced that a great many enterprises men commonly take for granted are merely desperate. He distrusted complexity and impedimenta as being the great thieves of time, and he believed that behind every man there rises and falls a tide that can float the British Empire like a chip."

"What the hell has the British Empire got to do with this?" asked my companion. "Was Thoreau an Anglophobe?"

"Not at all," I said. "He paid very little heed to governments—was preoccupied with the individual. He was particularly preoccupied with himself."

"I can see that. What else was eating him?"

"Well, he was suffering from the loss of a hound, a bay horse, and a turtledove."

"That sounds like sheer carelessness," replied the Senator. "Go ahead, what else was eating him?"

"He was a writer trying not to act like a writer," I continued. "He was a man possessed. He believed that the natural day was very calm; that if you followed your genius closely enough, it would not fail to show you a new prospect every hour. One of his friends described him as the captain of a huckleberry party—which I have always felt was a patronizing remark and not a very accurate one. It would be truer to say that Henry was the captain of a boarding party: he wanted to board men's minds, not to sell them a bill of goods, merely to assure them that the spirit is capable of elevation. The note he sounded was like the white-throat's—pure, wavering, full of the ecstasy of loneliness. He also advocated wearing old clothes when you had anything important to do."

"That's bad for business," mused the Senator. "The thing to do is keep producing more and better goods, and that includes clothing and accessories. What would happen if everybody just decided to wear their old clothes? There would be a slump."

"I know," I replied. "It's awfully confusing, and I sometimes wonder. Thoreau never bothered to systematize his philosophy—probably because he knew it had bugs in it; but you were asking about him, Senator, and I'm just filling you in. Henry was careful never to confuse the standard of living with the standard of furnishing. I mean, he foresaw Macy's basement, both its strength and its weakness, its bounty and its deception."

"Are you trying to tell me," roared McCarthy, "that the R. H. Macy Company is a fraud?"

"Quiet, Senator!" I said. "Nothing could be further from my intention or my belief. And let's not stray from the subject of this so interesting discussion. Thoreau felt that the ruts of tradition and conformity are deep; he spent a good deal of his life skirting them, for the pleasure of the sensation and the glory of man. He perceived that the life in us is like the water in a river—at any time it may rise to extravagant heights and drown out all our muskrats."

"I haven't *got* any muskrats!" yelled the Senator, who by this

49

time was thoroughly exasperated by the quality of my interpretation, as well as by the eccentricity of the author. With no attempt at concealing his irritation, he made a few notes, then put the notebook away and allowed his eyelids to droop. When I thought he wasn't looking, I pulled a bottle from my pocket, drew the stopper, and took a drink.

"Whuzzat?" asked the Senator.

"That," I said, "is a draught of undiluted morning air. You can find it on page 123." I offered him the bottle. He examined the label carefully.

"I never take a drink till after twelve o'clock."

"Then you're out of luck," I replied. "This stuff will not keep quite till noonday."

I could see that the Senator's curiosity was aroused. "Well," he said, grumblingly, "I might relax and try a little if it's non-alcoholic. Understand, I never take anything that makes me tipsy." He held the bottle to his lips and drained off a deep slug. The effect was immediate and terrible. McCarthy's eyes dilated. He stiffened. Perspiration broke from neck and forehead. The hostess of the plane, noticing his distress, came alongside to offer help. She took the bottle gently from his hand. When he spoke, the words came huskily.

"Throw away!" he croaked. "Poison!"

The hostess disappeared, carrying the fateful bottle.

When the plane reached New York, my companion was still in pain. He was barely able to thank me for my services as guide. The morning air, taken neat, had been overpowering: when one's system is long deprived of that elixir, which alone has the power to cure the general sickness, the shock of the first drink is great. The truth is, the journey had been almost too much for both of us. I think it may well be my last trip to the pond. Perhaps it was just because of the presence of the Senator, but the frogs sounded all the same as I listened—no variation in their voices. It didn't used to be that way, and I don't like such ponds.

4

Liberty

ANYTHING LIKE THAT

11/26/32

A YOUNG LADY, born in Russia, confided to us that she was about to become an American citizen, and would we be her witness, for she needed someone to testify to her good character and good intentions. Greatly touched, we dressed in a semiformal manner and accompanied her to a sort of barn over on the North River. Here we were tossed about from one United States naturalization clerk to another United States naturalization clerk, and eventually wound up before a bench, an American flag, and a grim, chilly examiner. After a few routine questions, the man suddenly speeded up his voice and inquired: "Do you believe in Communism, anarchism, polygamy—or anything like that?" And before we could pry into the phrase "anything like that"—which we felt it our duty to do—our young friend had blithely answered no, and it was all over. She is now an American citizen, a very pretty one, sworn never to believe in Anything Like That.

THE CONSTITUTION

2/8/36

THAT WAS A GOOD LETTER of Thomas Jefferson's which F. P. A.* published in his column, in which Jefferson pointed out that there was nothing sacred about constitutions, and that they were useful only if changed frequently to fit the changing needs of the people. Reverence for our Constitution is going to reach droll new heights this year; yet the Constitution, far from being a sacred document, isn't even a grammatical one. "We, the people of the United States, in order to form a more perfect union . . ." has turned many a grammarian's stomach, perfection being a state which does not admit of degree. A meticulous draughtsman would have written simply "in order to form a perfect union"—a thing our forefathers didn't dare predict, even for the sake of grammar.

POLITICAL SPEECHMAKING

7/8/44

THE THING WE REMEMBER of the Republican keynote speech, as it came in over the air, is the summer heat in the long grasses of the June night outside the window, and our own feeling of sin and of futility. It was the same feeling a boy has at the county fair, on the hot midway in the suggestive summertime, as he pauses before a barker outside a girl-show tent, with the smell of fried food in his nostrils and the enticements of girls in his mind, lost in the immemorial sheepishness of humanity and its deliberate exploitation by the ancient devices

---

*Franklin P. Adams's column "The Conning Tower" ran in *The New York World* and later in *The New York Herald Tribune*.

of oratory. The keynoter in Chicago indicated that the Republicans were against aggression, New Dealism, and the man-eating shark. There was to be no more aggression because Republicans do not tolerate any evil thing like aggression. The speaker gave no indication that the reorganization of a shattered world would require anything more than a mere extension of American culture and habits, as exemplified by past and present Republicans. In the summer night, we felt that we were a million boys, armed, bloody, and tired, standing and listening to this slick spiel, outside this gaudy and unlikely tent—listening and knowing all the while that we were about to be taken.

LIBERALISM

1/17/48

"THERE IS NO LIBERAL VIEW," sighed the *Herald Tribune* as the old year died, "no really self-consistent and logical body of principle and policy." It was a doleful thought, and the old year drew a few more tortured breaths and expired.

Ever since Thanksgiving, the *Herald Tribune* has been rassling with the theme of liberalism, and there have been mornings when the struggle resembled an old-fashioned rassling match with the Devil. The *Tribune*'s feeling about the independent liberal seems to be that he comes from a good family but has taken to hanging around pool halls. His instability, his shallow charm, his unpredictable movements, his dissolute companions, all have been the subject of speculation recently in the *Tribune*'s pages, and the word that was finally trotted out to describe his fate was the word "bankrupt." Even this word, however, seemed vaguely to trouble the *Tribune*, which does not in theory approve of any sort of American insolvency, even liberal insolvency. Clearly, a dilemma. The *Tribune* met it boldly by explaining that the liberal's work was done, his victory complete, and that henceforth the "conventional party structure" would be happy to carry the whole load and take care of the situation without any help. Its editorial paid tribute to the deep moral roots of nineteenth-century liberalism and the classic insurgencies, and traced the course of liberal history from the Jefferson revolt right down to the year 1933, at which point the editorialist gulped, hawked, and spat out.

The *Tribune*'s estimate of the independent liberal sounds to us a bit on the romantic side, a bit too full of the great tradition, not quite catching the essence of liberalism. The value of the liberal in the republic is not that he is logical but that he is inquisitive. At the moment, the liberal's desperate position and his dead life seem to us neither as desperate nor as dead as the *H. T.* has been making out. There are still a good many free men around who don't think that the liberal's work is done. (They would like to, but it isn't that easy.) The independent liberal, whether walking by his wild lone or running with a pack, is an essential ingredient in the two-party system in America—as strange and as vital as the trace elements in our soil. He gives the system its fluidity, its benign inconsistency, and (in cahoots with the major political organizations) its indisputable grace. We have never believed that the independent liberal had a priority on liberal thought, or a corner on the market; he merely lives in a semi-detached house and goes out without his rubbers. The *Tribune* itself has turned in such a good liberal performance lately in its news columns that its editorial shudders have seemed all the more strange. After all, it was the *Trib* that handed over ten columns last Sunday to William Z. Foster, who has seldom needed more than twenty-five words to hang himself in and this time did it in two flat, when he described legislative debates as "ridiculous talkfests."

The liberal holds that he is true to the republic when he is true to himself. (It may not be as cozy an attitude as it sounds.) He greets with enthusiasm the fact of the journey, as a dog greets a man's invitation to take a walk. And he acts in the dog's way, too, swinging wide, racing ahead, doubling back, covering many miles of territory that the man never traverses, all in the spirit of inquiry and the zest for truth. He leaves a crazy trail, but he ranges far beyond the genteel old party he walks with and he is usually in a better position to discover a skunk. The dog often influences the course the man takes, on his long walk; for sometimes a dog runs into something in nature so arresting that not even a man can quite ignore it, and the man deviates—a clear victim of the liberal intent in his dumb companion. When the two of them get home and flop down, it is the liberal—the wide-ranging dog—who is covered with burdocks and with information of a special sort on out-of-the-way places. Often ineffective in direct political action, he is the opposite of the professional revolutionary, for, unlike the latter, he never feels he knows where the truth lies, but is full of rich memories of places he has glimpsed it in. He is, on the whole, more optimistic than the revolutionary, or even than the Republican in a good year.

The *Tribune* may be right that there is no liberal "view." But the question is whether there is still a liberal spirit. In these melancholy days of Hooper and Gallup, when it is the vogue to belittle the thought in the individual and to glorify the thought in the crowd, one can only wonder. We think the spirit is there all right but it is taking a beating from all sides. Where *does* a liberal look these days? Mr. Truman has just suggested a forty-dollar bonus for all good taxpayers, Mr. Wallace has started calling people "ordinary" and man "common," and the *Herald Tribune* has liberalism on the mat, squeezing it in the kidneys. Your true liberal is on a spot, but it isn't the first time. Two dollars says it isn't going to be the last time. We'd make it five dollars except for all this talk of bankruptcy.

VOTER SANITY

ONE OF OUR OVERSEAS READERS has dropped us a line to inform us about the qualifications for voting in England. He got into a discussion with somebody in London about the matter, and they called the reference library of the House of Commons and received the following pronouncement: "In Great Britain any adult twenty-one years of age or over may register and vote except peers and lunatics. The latter, if they have a moment of lucidity, may register and vote." Our reader passed this on to us in the hope that it might sustain us through the difficult weeks ahead. The American political scene has seldom put such a strain on the sanity of the electorate, and we have an idea that when we step up to the polls next November we will feel like one of those British voters—daft as a coot, but praying, as we draw the curtain behind us, for a moment of lucidity.

A VOICE HEARD IN THE LAND

9/11/48

WE HAVE A CORDIAL INVITATION from the Businessmen for Wallace* to attend a dinner on the twenty-first, *couvert* $100, and although we ordinarily try to get to political rallies, we are hesitating on this one. The invitation shows a picture of Mr. Wallace in the act of delivering a speech, and there seems to be shining around him (and coming from above) a wonderful

---

*Henry A. Wallace, Progressive Party candidate for President in 1948. Originally a Republican, Wallace had been a Democrat as Secretary of Agriculture (1933–40), Vice President of the U.S. (1940–44), and Secretary of Commerce (1945–46).

radiance. It is probably a Consolidated Edison radiance, but there is nothing in the photograph to indicate that. This radiance looks like the real thing. Halfway down the shaft of light is a caption that says, "And a voice was heard in the land." The question that naturally arises, of course, is whether this land wants a voice. A distinguishing political feature of America is that it has never had a voice; it has had a lot of hoopdedoo but no voice, and that's the way we like it. Frankie Sinatra can handle the country's voice requirements, and the political candidates can handle the hoopdedoo, and we'll take ours without radiance, please.

Mr. Wallace has had a great deal to say about the infirmities and the unfairness of the American press, and we have taken most of his remarks lying down. He keeps saying that you can't learn the truth from the papers. We agree. You can't learn the truth from the papers. You can, however, buy at any newsstand a ten-cent assortment of biassed and unbiassed facts and fancies and reports and opinions, and from them you are allowed to try to assemble something that is a reasonable facsimile of the truth. And *that's* the way we like it, too. If a "voice" should ever be heard in the land, and stay heard, an awful lot of editorial pages and news pages would take the count. We think it entirely fair to remind the Businessmen of the most recent case where a voice was heard in a land. The voice was heard, the light came straight down from above, you could learn the Truth from the papers—and the land* is now under a four-power military government.

*Nazi Germany.

59

POLLING

THE TOTAL COLLAPSE of the public opinion polls* shows that this country is in good health. A country that developed an airtight system of finding out in advance what was in people's minds would be uninhabitable. Luckily, we do not face any such emergency. The so-called science of poll-taking is not a science at all but mere necromancy. People are unpredictable by nature, and although you can take a nation's pulse, you can't be sure that the nation hasn't just run up a flight of stairs, and although you can take a nation's blood pressure, you can't be sure that if you came back in twenty minutes you'd get the same reading. This is a damn fine thing.

Hollywood, which long ago elevated the pollster above the writer, and which invariably takes a blood count before beginning a picture, must be examining the results of the 1948 Presidential election with particular interest. Book clubs, which listen to the pitter-patter of millions of hearts before deciding whether a book is any good, must be studying the results, too. We are proud of America for clouding up the crystal ball, for telling one thing to a poll-taker, another thing to a voting machine. This is an excellent land. And we see even more clearly why the movies have advanced so slowly in the direction of art: Not only have the producers been deliberately writing down to the public but they've been getting bad information into the bargain. Who knows? Maybe the people aren't so far below them as they think.

*Polls had predicted Republican candidate Thomas Dewey's election, but Democratic candidate Harry Truman won despite competition from the Progressives (Henry Wallace) and Dixiecrats, which had threatened to drain Democratic votes.

SOCIAL SECURITY

11/20/48

PRESIDENT TRUMAN SAYS he is going to increase social security. By this he means that a somewhat larger amount will be
withheld from a worker's pay check each week and that the
employer will be asked to match the amount. Mark Sullivan, in
the *Tribune,* points out that with the value of money dropping
the way it is, an increase in social security is only an apparent
increase, not a real increase. Mr. Sullivan argues that the fifty
cents that was withheld from your pay check in, say, 1937
would have bought you a square meal at that time, but that
when you are sixty-five years old and get the fifty cents back,
it may buy you only a small box of dried raisins. He says the way
to increase social security is to see that the dollar doesn't shrink.
The argument is sound enough. Perhaps the way to manage
social security is to forget about dollars and withhold meat
instead. Every employer could be required to maintain a deep-
freeze unit and withhold one square meal each week for each
employee. Then when an employee reaches sixty-five and
starts digging around like a squirrel on a winter morning, he
will dig up some frozen meat instead of a shrivelled dollar. Of
course, withholding meat for security reasons would cause food
prices to skyrocket and this, too, might be a social advantage,
since many of us could normally be counted on to die of malnu-
trition before we ever reached sixty-five.

The problem of security is full of bewildering implications,
pitfalls, and myths. It is paradoxical that the more secure a
person gets in a material way, the less secure he may become
in other ways. The least secure fellows you see around, in any
age or period, are the big fellows, with their personal empires
and kingdoms and all the responsibilities and ulcers that go
with kinging. In a sense, the only genuinely secure person is a
healthy man possessed of absolutely nothing; such a man stands
aloof and safe—there is no way either to reduce his fortune or
to debase his currency. But even he is not perfectly secure: his
loneliness may suddenly depress his spirit, and this might en-
danger his health.
There is a sort of security in savagery, in that the savage

61

enjoys an extremely intimate and direct relationship with his supply—the berry, the root, the deermeat, the fish, the pelt. He is more truly a man of the world than is the civilized man. But he is not really secure, either; he soon notices the twinkle in a glass bead (and the possibilities of appreciation and exchange), and he fights wars with other savages (as do we all), and his security fades when the arrow is directed not at a deer but at another man.

OUR POLITICAL EXILES

8/6/49

A DOCUMENT DESCRIBING the Russian system of exile and forced labor has been produced by the British Government and is to be placed before the United Nations. It is estimated that some ten million persons in the Soviet Union are subject to compulsory work. These persons include the "unstable" elements, the "déclassé" elements. The concept of forced labor is so abhorrent to the American temperament, one wonders why there is so little concern in this country over our own system of forced idleness. The disease is the same—the difference is in the method of treating the victims. In the last couple of years, a handful of American citizens have been banished from industry for political reasons and forced into the camp of idleness. From this nucleus there can easily grow (and in fact there is growing) a group of American political prisoners. They are the "déclassé," the "unstable." Their crime is to have belonged to a wrong organization in a bygone year, to have once entertained a bubbly thought (or a second cousin at dinner), to have worn a hat backward, to have been seen by an agent at a rally. Industry is being encouraged to get shed of these unstable elements, these nebulous people. Laws are being framed to help detect and debar them. They may never have broken a law, or a piece of pottery, but they are being marched steadily, imperceptibly, toward the queer Siberia of our temperate zone. This is a dangerous exodus, an unhealthy state of mind. Perhaps a report should be placed before the U. N., but we would rather see it placed where it belongs—just a memo in the hatband of every democrat, reminding him that no country has a monopoly on political terror.

ORTHODOXY

12/30/50

FOR OURSELF, we shall resolve not to overwrite in the New Year, and to defend and exalt those principles and quirks that have carried the nation slowly up the long hill since it started: its gaiety, its resilience, its diversity, its tolerance of the divergent or the harassing idea, its respect for all men. Who is to say we are not greatly ascendant still? Because of fear, Americans have lately compromised their essential position—have published blacklists, have permitted legislative committees to presuppose what is "American," have watched them hang innocent men and women on the gallows of the newspaper headline, have winked at the meddling of congressmen in the conduct of the movies, have made the natural loyalty of the citizen ever so much more difficult by removing loyalty itself from the realm of free choice, have hinted that jobs belong chiefly to the confessed orthodox. For us, 1950 will be memorable above all other years because it was the year we once found ourself hesitating to throw something in the wastebasket, from a fleeting dread that it might be seen and misconstrued. In that one blinding moment of hesitation, the fresh air of America suddenly seemed contaminated with evil. The incident was absurd and the feeling passed, but nothing is quite absurd that happens.

Insofar as orthodoxy has gained strength, our republic has lost strength. But the loss is neither irreparable nor unusual. It is the product of war clouds—a sort of terrible mist that gathers. Luckily, many of our strongest skippers see through it. For 1951, we wish our readers health, faith, the sure eye that sees through mists, and the patience and muscle for the ascent of the most beautiful hill there is.

NEWSPAPER STRIKE

12/12/53

AT ONE POINT in the newspaper lull,* Edward R. Murrow remarked that "breakfast without a newspaper is a horse without a saddle"—an unhappy metaphor, it seemed to us. We began watching our own breakfasts, to see whether they were horses without saddles, and all we could discover was that the breakfast hour had achieved a sort of eerie serenity. Our digestion improved noticeably when the morning paper stopped arriving. Our private feeling about newspapers is a mixed one. Surely ninety per cent of all so-called news is old stuff—some of it two and three thousand years old. And surely ninety per cent of everything we read today is discouraging stuff, whether newsy or not. So the breakfast hour is the hour when we sit munching stale discouragement along with fresh toast. Except for one thing, we could take a newspaper or leave it alone. If we felt confident that liberty was secure and that democracy would remain in good health without assistance from its many admirers, we could do without a newspaper quite handily. At certain periods in our life, we've tried the experiment of not reading newspapers, and we found it put no strain on our system, since we enjoy a very low-grade curiosity and are seldom moved to keep informed of late developments. Mr. Murrow's famous opener, "This is the news," which carries the

*The International Photo-Engravers union was on strike against six New York newspapers from November 30 to December 9, 1953.

vox-humana sound of civilization-at-the-crossroads, often turns out to be a slight exaggeration. Nothing much happens from day to day. Public servants serve, felons act feloniously, demagogues croak their froggy tunes, echo answers echo (if it can get network time), and life goes on in its familiar pattern. But city dwellers without newspapers breathe an ominous air, as though the smog were descending. Liberty is not secure. Democracy does not thrive unassisted. And so, for love of these, we all swallow our bulletins at breakfast along with our marmalade.

WE'RE ALL AMERICANS

3/6/54

DR. SOCKMAN, the Methodist pastor, says the American city is more like a sand pile than a melting pot. "People are heaped together, but they do not hold together." Well, we have a letter telling us of an incident when Americans held together beautifully. The writer of the letter went, during his lunch hour, to buy stamps at the small post office in Bloomingdale's basement. Ahead of him in line was a lady who brought things to a standstill by changing her mind about what kind of stamps and envelopes she wanted, by running up a bill of more than thirty dollars, and by discovering that she didn't have thirty dollars and could she pay the balance by check? The line grew and grew. After a while, someone ventured to hope, out loud, that she wouldn't change her mind again, because he was on his lunch hour. At this, the woman turned on him and said, "You aren't even an American, are you?" The man was quite shaken by this, but the others in the line weren't, and they came to his aid instantly. "We're all Americans," shouted one of them, "and we are all on the lunch hour!"

That was no sand pile. People hold together and will continue to hold together, even in the face of abrupt and unfounded charges calculated to destroy.

A BUSY PLACE

Our Misfortunes in Canada, are enough to melt an Heart of Stone. The Small Pox is ten times more terrible than Britons, Canadians and Indians together. . . . There has been Want, approaching to Famine, as well as Pestilence. . . . But these Reverses of Fortune dont discourage me. It was natural to expect them, and We ought to be prepared in our Minds for greater Changes, and more melancholly Scenes still.

So wrote John Adams to Abigail, in one of his mercurial moments, June 26, 1776. We don't know how far into the future he was gazing, but if he were around today, celebrating our two-hundredth, he would not lack for melancholy scenes. As far as the eye can see in any direction, corruption and wrongdoing, our rivers and lakes poisoned, our flying machines arriving before the hour of their departure, our ozone layer threatened, our sea gasping for breath, our fish inedible, our national bird laying defective eggs, our economy inflated, our food adulterated, our children weaned on ugly plastic toys, our diversions stained with pornography and obscenity, violence everywhere, venery in Congress, cheating at West Point, the elms sick and dying, our youth barely able to read and write, the Postal Service buckling under the crushing burden of the mails and terrified by gloom of night, our sources of energy depleted, our railroads in decline, our small farms disappearing, our small businesses driven against the wall by bureaucratic edicts, and our nuclear power plants hard at work on plans to evacuate the countryside the minute something goes wrong. It is indeed a melancholy scene.

There is one thing, though, that can be said for this beleaguered and beloved country—it is alive and busy. It was busy in Philadelphia in 1776, trying to get squared away on a sensible course; it is busy in New York and Chillicothe today, trying to straighten out its incredible mess.

The word "patriot" is commonly used for Adams and for those other early geniuses. Today, the word is out of favor. Patriotism is unfashionable, having picked up the taint of chauvinism, jingoism, and demagoguery. A man is not expected to love his country, lest he make an ass of himself. Yet our country, seen through the mists of smog, is curiously lovable, in somewhat the way an individual who has got himself into an unconscionable scrape often seems lovable—or at least deserving of support. What other country is so appalled by its own shortcomings, so eager to atone for its own bad conduct? What other country ever issued an invitation like the one on the statue in New York's harbor? Wrongdoing, debauchery, decadence, decline—these are no more apparent in America today than are the myriad attempts to correct them and the myriad devices for doing it. The elms may be dying, but someone has developed a chemical compound that can be injected into the base of an elm tree to inhibit the progress of the disease. The Hudson River may be loaded with polychlorinated biophenyls, but there is an organization whose whole purpose is to defend and restore the Hudson River. It isn't as powerful as General Electric, but it is there, and it even gets out a little newspaper. Our food is loaded with carcinogens, while lights burn all night in laboratories where people are probing the mysteries of cancer. Everywhere you look, at the desolation and the melancholy scene, you find somebody busy with an antidote to melancholy, a cure for disease, a correction for misconduct. Sometimes there seems almost too much duplication of good works and therapeutic enterprise; but at least it suggests great busyness—a tremendous desire to carry on, against odds that, in July of 1976, as in June of 1776, often seem insuperable.

> But these Reverses of Fortune dont discourage me. . . . It is an animating Cause, and brave Spirits are not subdued with Difficulties.

Let us, on this important day when the tall ships move up the poisoned river, take heart from good John Adams. We might even for a day assume the role of patriot, with neither apology nor shame. It would be pleasant if we could confront the future with confidence, it would be relaxing if we could pursue happiness without worrying about a bad fish. But we are stuck with our chemistry, our spraymongers, our raunchy and corrupt public servants, just as Adams was stuck with the Britons, the Canadians, the Indians, and the shadow of Small Pox. Let not the reverses discourage us—liberty is an animating Cause (and there's not much smallpox around, either). If the land does not unfold fair and serene before our eyes, neither is this a bad place to be. It is unquestionably a busy one. Bang the bell! Touch off the fuse! Send up the rocket! On to the next hundred years of melancholy scenes, splendid deeds, and urgent business!

5

Maine

COME ONE, COME ALL

8/26/44

THERE ARE MANY FACETS of the promotional spirit which beguile us, but our favorite is the promotion of states of the Union by their development commissions. It is common practice for a state to recommend itself as a sanctuary to people of other states, extending a blanket invitation to all to come and romp in the peculiar sunlight within its borders. Maine, conscious of its paradisiacal quality, doggedly advertises its "unspoiled wilderness," presumably in the hope that millions will shortly arrive to cry in it. This is an odd quirk. Obviously, if a state valued its wildness, it would keep silent and not let the secret out among the tame. The very idea of "development" is inconsistent with natural beauty, and there is, of course, little likelihood that the Maine woods will be thoroughly appreciated by Maine until after they no longer exist, except in the joists and rafters of the wayside soft-drink parlors.

Bill Geagan, a sportswriter for the Bangor *News,* wrote a column the other day in strong contrast to the rich prose of the vacation ads. He was describing a Maine trout stream before the black flies entered the scene to distract his attention: "I found unsightly dumps that contained rusted bedsprings, tin cans, automobile seats and tires, iron wagon-wheel tires, burlap sacks, washtubs, barrel hoops, medicine and beer bottles, rotten potatoes, and wornout corsets. . . . It should be remembered that the future of this great State of ours . . ."

And so on. Nowadays the journey a man makes to escape from his own rusty bedsprings is a long one, and in every coppice lurks a development commission.

BLENDING IN

1/13/45

THE GERMANS, who do things well up to a certain point, made two serious mistakes in their latest attempt to land saboteurs in this country. They picked Maine, which was one mistake. And they dressed the lads in topcoats, which was another. Maine people, as young Master Hodgkins pointed out, don't wear topcoats in winter. In that cold climate the topcoat has long been recognized as a fraudulent garment—open at the sleeves, open at the neck, open at the bottom, drafty as a north chamber. The spies were immediately spotted as "from away."

The coast of Maine, viewed from a chart, must have seemed to the Germans the perfect place to put someone ashore—a long coastline, rocky, wooded, and difficult. But the people who live in the villages on Maine's coast are members of the oldest bureau of investigation in existence—they have the eyes, the ears, and the curiosity of hunters and fishers, and whatever or whoever comes ashore or goes afloat, man, bird, or beast, in whatever kind of weather, is duly noted and entered in the book of days.

Probably Germans like to do things the hard way. They get a kick out of running a submarine into an American bay in a snowstorm and unloading a couple of spy-school graduates carrying invisible ink, who later turn up at a table in Leon & Eddie's. A more sensible, and much simpler, way to get saboteurs into this country would be to parachute them down into Bryant Park at high noon, in fancy clothes, from a plane trailing a streamer advertising a Broadway show. The cops would chalk it up to press-agentry, and after the spies had satisfied a couple of autograph hounds, they could walk away and proceed to the serious business of blowing up the Kensico Dam and releasing the lions from the Zoo.

PULPWOOD

9/4/48

WE WERE BAITING a flounder hook with a clam belly the other afternoon when we looked up and saw an LCT* entering the cove. For an instant we thought perhaps things had started up all over again, but when the captain dropped anchor and cut his engine, we could hear a baby cry and, as the craft swung to the wind, could see that there were no tanks aboard. An hour or two later, when the tide served, the anchor came up and the boat headed for the beach—straight at a pile of pulpwood. The ramp rattled down, a truck appeared from the woods, and in short order the landing craft was being loaded with pulpwood, presumably for the nearest paper mill, which is owned by Time, Inc. The operation continued for about an hour. When the tide turned, the ramp came up. The captain backed away and anchored again in deep water. Darkness and mosquitoes enfolded the gaunt black hull. We noticed that, like some of the sentences in *Time,* she lay stern to the wind.

Early next morning the craft hit the beach again and resumed loading pulpwood. It was an awesome sight, this tentacle of empire reaching out into so remote and quiet a spot; and it was a fearsome sound, the throbbing engines of an old, dead war furnishing the paper for new conquests in the magazine field. Awesome or not, the LCT proved a handy rig for loading pulpwood, and a pleasant visitor in the cove. We got one flounder. Luce got, we should judge, about sixty cord.

*Landing Craft Tank. See pp. 298–99 in *Letters of E. B. White* for letters discussing this piece. After he wrote it, White found out that the landing craft was headed not for the mill at Bucksport, Maine owned by Time-Life, but rather for a mill in Brewer, Maine.

LATE AUGUST

9/3/49

FOR US THE PRETTIEST DAY in all the long year is the day that comes unexpectedly at the end of August in the country. It is a cool day, freshly laundered (as though straight from the Bendix* of the gods), when the airs, the light, and a new sound from the grasses give the world a wholly changed character. On this day, summer, languishing but not really sick, receives her visitors with a certain deliberateness—a pretty girl who knows she doesn't need to stay in bed. The yellow squash illuminates the aging vine, the black-billed cuckoo taps out his hollow message in code (a series of three dots), and zinnias stand as firm and quiet as old valorous deeds. This is the day the farmer picks up the first pullet egg, a brown and perfect jewel in the grass; the day a car stops and a man gets out and tacks up a poster advertising the county fair. You couldn't get us to swap this one day for any six other days.

CHANGE OF SEASON

10/13/51

THE CHANGE-OF-SEASON EDITOR of *Time* sat down the other day, closed his eyes, opened them again, and wrote his mood piece on the coming of autumn to the U. S. The piece was headed "Stain in the Air." "Autumn," said *Time,* "came to the U. S. last week with a souse of wet snow on Denver, a spatter of cold rain on South Dakota's Black Hills, a chill wind in Chicago that moved on to New York. . . . It was a time of transition and suspension. Along New England's shores, the squeak of a

---

*Bendix Home Appliance Co. produced home laundry equipment.

fisherman's oars against thole pins sounded lonely and clear in the fog of early morning. . . . On the Pacific Coast, nights had turned cold. . . . In Texas river bottoms the sweet gum trees were tinged with yellow." Then followed a quick estimate of UStemper* at applefall, ending, "In the uneasy air of 1951's autumn, a sense of wrong stained the air like smog."

This piece, ranging so widely and concluding so sadly, depressed us, and we felt wave after wave of Wrongsense lapping at our shingle. But right in the middle of feeling so bad we realized that, by a lucky chance, we were in an excellent position to check one of *Time*'s items—the one about the squeak of a fisherman's oars against thole pins along New England's shores. We just happened to *be* on a New England shore; furthermore, the hour was early and the morning was foggy. Cocking our ears, we soon picked up the sounds made by a departing fisherman. What we heard, of course, was first the scraping of the conventional galvanized rowlock in its galvanized socket, then, a few moments later, the crisp explosions of a six-cylinder Chevrolet conversion, whose cheerful pistons were soon delivering more thrusts per minute than there are thole pins in all of Maine. The collapse of this single *Time* item when checked against the facts restored our sense of well-being, and we went in to breakfast wondering whether those Texas sweet-gum trees were tinged with yellow or with robin's-egg blue.

*Time magazine frequently coined words in this manner. But that was not their only sin. Retaliating for *Fortune*'s 1934 profile of *The New Yorker*, Wolcott Gibbs in a parody profile of Henry Luce, *Time*'s editor, imitated *Time*'s inversion of normal sentence structure: "Backward ran sentences until reeled the mind."

6

One World

INIMICAL FORCES

4/8/33

EINSTEIN IS LOVED because he is gentle, respected because he is wise. Relativity being not for most of us, we elevate its author to a position somewhere between Edison, who gave us a tangible gleam, and God, who gave us the difficult dark and the hope of penetrating it. Not long ago Einstein was here and made a speech, not about relativity but about nationalism. "Behind it," he said, "are the forces inimical to life." Since he made that speech we have been reading more about those forces: Bruno Walter forbidden by the Leipzig police to conduct a symphony; shops of the Jews posted with labels showing a yellow spot on a black field. Thus in a single day's developments in Germany we go back a thousand years into the dark, while a great thinker, speaking not as Jew but as philosopher, warns us: these are the forces inimical to life.

COMMON ENEMY

10/12/35

STATESMEN AND HISTORIANS have long known that a common enemy is the most solidifying thing a nation can have, welding all the people into a happy, united mass. We saw how true that was in our own home last week when we discovered that the place we had moved into had cockroaches, or, as the cook calls them, cackaroachies. We discovered them late one night when we went down into the pantry and snapped on a light; since then, the household has warred against them with a high feeling of family unity and solidarity, sniping at them with a Flit gun, rubbing poisonous paste on bits of potatoes for them to eat, the house full of great singleness of purpose and accord. No wonder a dictator, when he feels uneasy, looks around for something for his people to squash.

SCRAP IRON

4/3/37

OLD, DEAD AUTOMOBILES, moldering in roadside grave-yards, have long been a worrisome sight in this country. We peer into glade and glen, and find bodies decomposing there, stripped of tires and batteries. Foreigners, visiting us, are appalled at the spectacle, and write letters home to their papers about American wealth and waste. But today these carcasses lie uneasily in their burial grounds, preyed upon by grave robbers of a new sort. The price of scrap iron and steel has risen tremendously—it seems there is a European demand: iron is wanted for the wars, and the stealthy junkman arrives to pluck the ancient Overland from the caress of raspberry vine and nettle. At his approach, field mice flee their nest in the cushions. Iron for the wars! Somewhere a peasant saves his broken spade for the government collector; somewhere a bride melts down her wedding ring for God and country; somewhere someone's old family sedan goes to its great adventure. The iron we could not quite destroy will serve destruction yet. Scrap iron, scrap steel, scrap gold. Scrap life.

VIGIL

THIS WILL BE ONE OF THOSE mute paragraphs written despite the impossible interim of magazine publication, handed over to a linotyper who has already heard later news. Today is Sunday, August 27th. Perhaps you don't remember that far back, you who presumably now dwell in a world which is either at peace or at war. It is three o'clock in the morning. The temperature in New York is 70 degrees, sky overcast. The long vigil at the radio is beginning to tell on us. We have been tuned in, off and on, for forty-eight hours, trying to snare intimations of our destiny, as in a butterfly net. Destiny, between musical transcriptions. We still twitch nervously from the likelihood of war at 86 on the dial to the possibility of peace at 100 on the dial. The hours have induced a stupor; we glide from Paris to London to Berlin to Washington—from supposition to supposition, lightly. (But that wasn't a supposition, that was the Hotel Astor.) The war of nerves, they call it. It is one of those phrases that catch on. Through it all the radio is immense. It is the box we live in. The world seems very close at hand. ("Countless human lives can yet be saved.") We sit with diners at the darkened tables in the French cafés, we pedal with the cyclists weekending in the beautiful English countryside, we march alongside the German troops approaching the Polish border, we are a schoolboy slipping on his gas mask to take shelter underground from the raid that hasn't come, we sit at the elbow of Sir Neville* as he presents the message to the British Cabinet (but what does it say?). Hour after hour we experience the debilitating sensation of knowing everything in the world except what we want to know—as a child who listens endlessly to an adult conversation but cannot get the gist, the one word or phrase that would make all clear. The world, on this Sunday morning, seems pleasingly unreal. We've been reading (between bulletins) that short story of Tomlinson's called "Illusion: 1915," which begins on a summer day in France when the bees

---

*Neville Chamberlain, Prime Minister of Great Britain 1937–40. His policies of appeasement of the Germans ("peace in our time") such as the 1938 Munich Pact, though supported by many at the time, failed to discourage Hitler's expansionism.

were in the limes. But this is Illusion 1939, this radio sandwich on which we chew, two bars of music with an ominous voice in between. And the advertiser, still breaking through: "Have you acquired the safety habit?" Moscow is calling New York. Hello, New York. Let me whisper I love you. They are removing the pictures from the museums. There was a time when the mere nonexistence of war was enough. Not any more. The world is in the odd position of being intellectually opposed to war, spiritually committed to it. That is the leaden note. If war comes, it will be war, and no one wants that. If peace is restored, it will be another arrangement enlarging not simply the German boundary but the Hitler dream. The world knows it can't win. Let me whisper I love you while we are dancing and the lights are low.*

SUPREMACY

3/27/43

THE LEAST SATISFYING ESSAY we have seen on the subject of isolation was written by an advertising man for an airplane company. He described the shrinking of the world, the ease with which anyone could hop from one point on the earth to any other point. He concluded with the curious observation that, the world being what it is today, the United States should see to it that it (the U.S.) achieves unquestioned supremacy of the air in the postwar world.

This conclusion, mystical and spooky though it is, seems to be a fairly common one. We find it hard to arrive at, either logically or superstitiously. If it appears necessary to an American that America should assume control of the air, then presumably

*Germany invaded Poland on September 1, 1939. Great Britain and France declared war on Germany on September 3.

it seems necessary to an Englishman that England should, and to a Russian that Russia should, and to a German that Germany should. The postwar world thus becomes simply an extension of the prewar world, same rules, same outlook. We should all get out our little book on logic and study hard. The answer must be in there somewhere.

LIBERATION OF PARIS

9/2/44

PROBABLY ONE OF THE DULLEST stretches of prose in any man's library is the article on Paris in the Encyclopædia Britannica. Yet when we heard the news of the liberation, being unable to think of anything else to do, we sat down and read it straight through from beginning to end. "Paris," we began, "capital of France and of the department of Seine, situated on the Ile de la Cité, the Ile St. Louis, and the Ile Louviers, in the Seine, as well as on both banks of the Seine, 233 miles from its mouth and 285 miles S. S. E. of London (by rail and steamer via Dover and Calais)." The words seemed like the beginning of a great poem. A feeling of simple awe overtook us as we slowly turned the page and settled down to a study of the city's weather graph and the view of the Seine looking east from Notre Dame. "The rainfall is rather evenly distributed," continued the encyclopædist. Evenly distributed, we thought to ourself, like the tears of those who love Paris.

U. N. ARROW

4/20/46

THE SUBTLEST SIGN in town is on an "L" pillar at Forty-eighth Street and Third Avenue. The sign reads, "UNITED NATIONS," and there is an arrow. The arrow is vertical—one of those conventional highway "straight ahead" indications. A hurried motorist probably would interpret this without trouble and would keep going toward the East River Drive; but we were on foot, and far gone in meditation, and for us the arrow distinctly pointed straight up past the dingy railroad tracks and on into Heaven.

THE UNIVERSAL THEME

4/3/48

THE RESURRECTION IS VISIBLE in the back yard in the green spear breaking ground, and it is audible in the choirs in the churches. The sparrow selects a piece of dull string for the resurrection; the stroller selects a bright necktie. The zealot overhauls his set of ideas and finds rebirth in running his fingers through them, as the gardener takes strength from touching the earth. The theme of freedom emerges like a woodchuck after a long winter of cold and crisis, and is reborn under sombre skies.

Out at Lake Success,* the peepers celebrate love and the unity of earth, the talkers celebrate hate and division. Professor Cantril, of Princeton, has been named by Unesco† to inquire into tensions and to study ways to stimulate respect among

---

*Meeting place for the United Nations.
†Unesco: United Nations Educational, Scientific, and Cultural Organization.

nations for each other's ideals. He will examine influences that predispose toward nationalism. He will be a busy man. Almost everything one reads and hears these days predisposes toward nationalism; only the peepers and the green spears publish the universal theme. The nation steams like a cup of hot coffee, and the patriot's spectacles become fogged, so that he sees nothing except through the mind's eye, merely feels the strong, warm liquid going into his stomach, stimulating his glands.

In Town Hall the other night, at a radio forum, we heard a man in the audience address the moderator: "Isn't it true, sir, that in the last analysis this boils down to the old struggle between freedom and tyranny?" All around him heads nodded gratefully, everyone relieved to have life clarified in a moment of revelation. Anti-Communism is strong drink. Already the lines are being drawn tighter; already fear produces symptoms of the very disease we hope to fight off: the preoccupation with loyalty, the tightening of censorship, the control of thought by legislative committee, the readiness to impute guilt by association, the impatience with liberalism. The tyrant fear, pricking us to fight tyranny. This time, we suspect, there is more on the stage than the old familiar conflict between freedom and tyranny. The playwright is subtly ambitious and carries another theme along, and we are about to witness the death scene of nationalism to boot. This is the big act, and we who live in this decade are the favored few.

A week or two ago, in *Life,* Dorothy Thompson published a letter she had from Jan Masaryk,* whose suicide pointed the dilemma of millions of free-spirited men who find themselves in circumstances for which they feel partially responsible and from which they see no escape. The letter revealed Masaryk's self-doubts and his presentiment of the spiritual impasse toward which he was headed. It was dated November 15th. "I have been toying with the idea," he wrote, "to let myself go at one of the closing sessions of the General Assembly and call out a warning to all those self-centered nationalists assembled in

*Masaryk, Czechoslovakian minister for foreign affairs, represented Czechoslovakia at the San Francisco Conference of the United Nations in 1945 and managed to remain in power after the Communist coup in February 1948. He died March 10, 1948, from a fall from an apartment window in Prague; the Communist government announced it as a suicide.

the 'Flushing-Success' area. It is the question of timing that worries me."

He did not let himself go, and no one is wise enough to say whether his timing would have been good or bad. But most of us can feel something of the paralysis of that doubt, something of the pulsation of that intent.

The essential antagonism between the Russian world and the Western world is in the emphasis each places on responsibility. Both capitalism and socialism accept certain responsibilities, avoid others. Socialism holds itself responsible to the people for the use and management of resources, and in so doing is likely to wind up (as it has in Russia) by managing everything, including the citizen's private life, his thoughts, his arts, and his science. This is wholly repugnant to democratic capitalists, whose system accepts the responsibility for guarding civil liberties and is notably cavalier about private concentrations of economic power, despite the fact that the destinies of the people are tied up in them. And so the antagonism grows—each system both ambitious and fearful, largely because of the presence of the other. The argument about responsibility seems ready to boil over into a mess that, for utter *ir*responsibility, would make the gaudiest robber barons of capitalism and the most ruthless tyrants of Communism look like pikers.

The question of responsibility is a pervasive one. The United Nations, lacking both money and force, and being merely a set of nations with their fingers crossed, has not been able to assume much responsibility for humanity. The "self-centered nationalists" whom Jan Masaryk hesitated to warn are not all of them deliberately self-centered, but the Charter offers little chance for any delegate to be anything but centered on self and nation.

We recommend to Professor Cantril, in his search for things that predispose toward nationalism, that he reexamine the principles of the Charter. The Charter specifies "coöperation." Yet small nations coöperate reluctantly and big nations do not coöperate at all. The Charter advertises "sovereign equality." But equality is a myth. A voting procedure based on equality is an exasperation to strong nations and not much comfort to weak ones. Ask any western European nation about its sovereign equality when the shadow of Russian expansion stretches across it from the east and the gleam of American dollars strikes it from the west. Ask the ghost of Masaryk. The Charter seeks collective security by the prevention of aggression, but nobody has ever figured out how to prevent aggression by disciplining nations, and we are all less secure, singly and collectively, than we were three years ago.

It seems to us that the people of our country and of many other countries believe in the purposes of the United Nations but are baffled and discouraged by its principles. As long as we're an independent nation, we have to pursue a national policy. But if the people say so, our foreign policy can be broadened to express a universal principle even while acting to preserve a national ideal. Anti-Communism is our necessary foreign policy at the moment, but it is negative and it is incomplete. The long-term policy of the United States should be to end the anarchy of sovereign states and to build the government of free people. We ask the delegates to take a stroll some evening, leave the hall and go over to the lake, and listen to the lovesick little frog, *Hyla crucifer,* for the sound of the correct principle.

EAGLES AND BEARS

11/26/49

MR. McNEIL* AND MR. VISHINSKY exchanged fables last week, thereby charming the United Nations with a fresh obliquity of expression. We were glad to see this trend, and we commend to the delegates the fable of the Raccoon and the Fresh-Water Mussel. It goes like this:

*Hector McNeil, Minister of State for Great Britain, headed the British delegation to the U. N. Andrei Y. Vishinsky was Foreign Minister of the U.S.S.R.

After the long bloodiness of the jungle, the animals assembled their delegates in the council place to put an end to the scourge of trouble and to establish a community of beasts, devoid of tooth and fang, free from the legacy of fear. Delegates were soon making speeches, among the longest of which were the speeches of the Bear, the Eagle, and the Lion.

"It is quite clear," said the Bear, pounding the table with his paw, "that the Eagles are up to no good. Everything Eagles do is warlike and wrong. Lions are bad, too. The jungle would be an excellent place if all animals would act more like Bears and would turn matters over to the head Bear. Bears are the thing."

The animals listened attentively to this speech and the Raccoon applauded loudly. Then the Eagle rose and opened his beak.

"The trouble with Bears," said he, "is that they keep too much to themselves. I would like to see Bears mingle more. Because a Bear likes raspberries, it doesn't mean *I* like raspberries. Because Bears sleep in winter, must an Eagle who stays awake be called stupid?"

"Good speech," said the Lion. "Jolly good. Furthermore, time runs out."

There followed a few other speeches by minor animals and then the delegates withdrew to their personal jungles.

The first to get home was the Eagle.

"What happened?" asked all the Eagles.

"If you were listening to your radios, you know what happened," answered the Eagle. "There will be a rebroadcast at ten-thirty this evening for anybody who missed the proceedings."

The Lion was the second to get home.

"What happened?" asked all the Lions.

"Here—read all about it," said the Lion, handing them copies of the London *Times*.

The Bear was the last to get home.

"What happened?" asked all the Bears.

"Well," said the Bear, "I simply told the other animals how the Eagles and the Lions were preparing for war. I explained that the jungle would be all right if everybody would be more like Bears and would turn things over to the head Bear. I made it clear that Bears are the thing."

"What did the others say to that?" asked the delighted Bears.

"What did they say?" said the Bear. "Say? Why, they said the same old stuff. What they said was propaganda. You Bears don't need to know what they said, because it is without meaning." And the old Councilbear smiled. That night, when some of the more inquisitive of the Bears turned on their radios, all they heard in their radio sets was the sighing of the wind in the treetops.

The debate continued for several months. Each jungle session saw the Bears, the Lions, and the Eagles at odds. After each session, the Council-animals returned and made their familiar reports. Once in a while a very small animal would make a speech—a Chipmunk, or a Water Beetle—but nobody paid much attention. Everyone concentrated on Lions, Bears, and Eagles.

The Eagles worried so much about what the Bears were doing they got ulcers. Some Eagles had to sip milk in the middle of the morning. It was humiliating. The Bears, on the other hand, worried about what the Eagles were up to. The more they worried, the closer they kept to themselves. They would sleep for months at a time, hibernating, in the wintertime of fear.

The Eagles, sensing trouble, sharpened their talons and stockpiled steel toenails. The Bears, sensing trouble, sharpened their teeth and stockpiled brass claws. Everyone in the jungle was acutely unhappy, except, of course, the Chickadees, who never allowed anything to depress them. The small animals were restless, realizing that the jungle was overburdened with strong Bears lying low, strong Eagles flying high. It was a bad situation. However, things weren't impossible. Bears didn't really dislike Eagles, and the Eagles didn't really dislike Bears. It was all on paper—or in the mind.

It wasn't till the day a Raccoon ate a Fresh-Water Mussel that the lid blew off.

"You can't do that to a Mussel!" screamed an Eagle.

"Why not?" asked the Raccoon, who had acted on impulse.

"Because it's unkind and because I have an arrangement with Fresh-Water Mussels," said the Eagle.

"Never heard of it," said the Raccoon.

"Well, lay off Fresh-Water Mussels! Who strikes a Fresh-Water Mussel strikes me!" screamed the Eagle. "Death to Raccoons!"

"O.K.," said the Raccoon, "death to Eagles!"

"This concerns me," said the Bear. "Raccoons are my little

brothers. Who strikes a Raccoon strikes me. Death to the people who strike Raccoons!"

"O.K.," cried the Eagles, who were immediately joined by the Lions, "death to Raccoons *and* Bears!"

In almost no time, the Bears and the Eagles and the Lions tangled, and were joined by Water Beetles, Chipmunks, Moles, Luna Moths, Porcupines, Jackals, Ladybugs, Sloths, Barn Swallows, and Whirling Mice. It was a mess. The Eagles and the Bears were the only ones that had real power, and they fixed everything quick. For the next three or four million years, the jungle was silent and relaxed. Only the sound of the wind disturbed it—and the small whirring noise in some of the radio sets abandoned by the dead Bears.

SNOWSTORMS

12/22/51

THERE WAS A FLURRY OF SNOW one morning recently—a sudden gaiety and white charm at breakfast time, the snow descending prettily across roof and wall. The moment we saw this cheerful sight, this unexpected bonus, our mind rocketed back to a time in childhood, a morning unforgettable because of snow. The snow that day arrived in blizzard force; at eight o'clock the fire siren, muffled by the blast, wailed the "No School Today" signal, and we retired in ecstasy to a warm attic room and to Meccano. The thing we remember is the coziness, the child's sense of a protective screen having been quickly drawn between him and his rather frightening world. This feeling was perfectly reproduced for us the other morning. For about five minutes, the snow seemed quite capable of insulating us from all harm, from every trouble, from evil itself, and we were again in the warm, safe attic with a straightforward problem in mechanical engineering.

The Russians are trying, with their curtain, to draw the protective screen and make it snow forever in the world, for their special benefit. They long for the sense of security that circumstances and their own stubbornness have denied them. A childish surrender to unreality, the curtain not only does not shut out evil, it *is* evil. The curtain is not merely the screen that makes it impossible for the West to relax its arms, it is itself the core of Russian armament. It is poison gas in political form.

There ought to be a healthy debate going on today—a debate between capitalism and socialism, between individualism and statism. The curtain has prevented this debate from taking place, and although there is plenty of talk in the forum, we are really stuck with the fact of having no discussion. The Russians do not qualify as debaters, because they have boxed their argument, sealed their people, and turned out the house lights. In consequence, the delegates to the United Nations stand around and talk about peace and disarmament—subjects on which there is no real difference of opinion. (Everybody loves peace by the terms of the contract, and nobody can risk disarming under the conditions created by the curtain.)

An interesting experiment would be to place the curtain itself on the agenda. It is not a secondary matter, to be buried in committee; it is the big thing. The U. N. cannot much longer pretend that questions can be genuinely discussed under Russia's terms—with all ideas being halted at the border, with writers being instructed how to write, with radio being jammed. Such "discussions" are farcical, and are quite expensive, too. The United States has proposed that the curtain be opened just enough to allow inspectors to walk through and look about for concealed weapons. That begs the issue. The free nations of the U. N. should ask Russia to show cause why her curtain should not be abandoned—not as an approach to disarmament but as a precondition of further debate on anything at all. The curtain is the one topic that must acutely embarrass the Soviet lords, it is such a telltale device: evidence of their fear, symbol of their immaturity, and sure sign of their contempt for people. The curtain is their private snowstorm, behind which they hope to withdraw and play with their construction set.

PIRANHAS

THERE'S A TROPICAL-FISH STORE in this vicinity, and one of the tanks contains a solitary piranha—a little fish that looks something like a sunfish. The price tag says $25—quite a sum for a three-inch pet that sulks in a watery corner, slowly waving its pectorals. However, the piranha has this to be said for it: it is a man-eater. Fierce, remorseless, and with a taste for the flesh of warm-blooded animals, it will attack furiously. We pass the fish store almost every day on our way to work, the blood flowing warm in our veins, the prospect of another day at a typewriter filling our head with suicidal fancies, and we always stop for a moment in front of the piranha. We like having a murderous fish in the neighborhood; it is reassuring to know that all we have to do is dive into a nearby tank to be stripped flesh from bone in a matter of minutes.

A glance at the calendar, a glimpse of Gristede's,* set us exploring our private reserves of gratitude and adoration. To forget the world's abundance, even briefly and in a moment of spiritual penury, is to lose one's toehold on the ladder. The sun rises, the leaves fall, the park grows cold, the springs flow, the birds rip by on knowing wings, the pumpkin accedes to the throne, and men prepare. For what do they prepare? Unlike birds, trees, sun, they prepare for war—or else they prepare for they know not what, which is almost the same thing. They prepare, perhaps, for cold. Fearing the worst, they prepare for the worst. But there is still room for thanks—not for the pass we've reached but for the setting against which we've reached it, a backdrop beyond compare, a scene of wild and illimitable promise, a revolutionary cyclorama of cleverly concealed progress, with good men holding firm. Wanted: a third act. Until we know that the playwright has collapsed or gone in with the piranha, until we know that all's behind, we shall innocently assume that all is ahead, and render thanks, at the customary time and in the customary way, for the privilege of a walk-on part in the show.

*Chain of food stores.

CITIZEN OF THE WORLD

12/19/53

OUT IN SUMMIT, NEW JERSEY, the students of the Junior High recite a school pledge at their assemblies, and the pledge used to start, "I, a student of Summit Junior High School and a future citizen of the world, promise to obey and uphold the laws of my country and school." The Veterans of Foreign Wars got wind of this dangerous condition and persuaded the school authorities to strike out the offensive phrase "citizen of the world." The school children must, therefore, have been surprised the other day when the same phrase popped up in President Eisenhower's address to the United Nations. "The atomic age," he said, "has moved forward at such a pace that every citizen of the world should have some comprehension, at least in comparative terms, of the extent of this development." Clear case of the President of the United States going over the heads of the Veterans of Foreign Wars. We don't know what the next step of the school authorities should be—give up assemblies, perhaps, as being a breeding ground for difference of opinion.

FRIENDSHIP CARDS

6/19/54

A GREETING-CARD FIRM has sent us some statistics about the expression of friendship and good will in America. The figures are staggering. In 1953, some three and a half billion cards were mailed, carrying greetings of one sort or another. Friendships ranked high on the list, along with Get Well Soons, Happy Birthdays, and Merry Andsoforths. For a firm dealing in the emotions of love and affection, the statistician's mind runs on very strange matters indeed. Thus we read that the money spent on "friendship" in 1953 would "pay for a battleship." And if stacked one atop another in their envelopes, those three and a half billion messages of love would "make a pile so high that even the Russians couldn't invent a guided missile that could get over the top of it. It would be 4,375 miles up in the ionosphere." There seems to be something wrong here somewhere. Perhaps we should simply stack these friendship cards instead of mailing them, thus warding off unfriendly missiles. Or perhaps we're sending cards to the wrong people. Why doesn't some enterprising greeting-card firm get up a mailing list of our "enemies" (there must be billions of them), to whom a friendship card would come as a real surprise? The money spent on the cards would still pay for a battleship, but if the cards worked, the battleship might never have to open fire.

HUNGARIAN REVOLT

12/22/56

A FEW YEARS AGO, when Joseph Stalin was still alive, we tried to write a Christmas allegory in the form of a playlet. It didn't come off. But we are reminded of it this year because of recent events in Europe. Our story was about a Russian emissary to the United States who goes back to his homeland at Christmas to check in. As a gag, he brings Stalin a gift of a luminous candy cane from America. The cane arouses the Marshal's curiosity. He pumps his man about life in the United States, and the two of them have a few drinks. Stalin wants to know what Christmas is like over here. He asks to be filled in on the story of the Nativity, and the emissary tells it, rather blunderingly. Stalin wants to know why the candy cane shines. "They doctor it up with something, I guess," the fellow says. The two men get a bit drunk. And before the underling leaves, he tells his boss that, actually, it isn't just candy canes that act this way. A lot of things in America seem to be sort of luminous; things just get looking lighter than they should—streets, buildings, the sky, the faces of little girls in the park when they buy the popcorn and the pigeons fly up and the wings of birds are all around them. The emissary leaves after a while. Stalin is furious at the inadequacy of the man's explanation, the rambling tale of unexplained luminosity. The room grows dark. The cane, hanging on a hat tree, shines in the gloom, a bright inverted J. Finally, after making several attempts to eat the cane and being scared off by the possible consequences, he rings for an aide and orders the hated object removed. He tells the aide to bury the cane—secretly, so none shall see the light from it.

As you can gather from the synopsis, this wasn't much of an allegory. But now, in 1956, at Christmas, a candy cane does indeed hang in the Kremlin on the hat tree. The cane is a luminous one, and sheds the old, disturbing, familiar light. It is of Hungarian manufacture,* brought back by an emissary, and not as any gag, either. The presence of this object gives the 1956 Christmas a different look from any Christmas the world has had in a long, long while. Mr. Stalin is dead, and few are the mourners. His successors, the heads of state, will be afraid to eat this luminous cane, because of the mysterious nature of its ingredients, and they will be unable to get a satisfactory explanation of what makes it shine. (The light generated by men on their way toward freedom has never been really explained.) And even though the heads of state bury the disagreeable object, which they will surely try to do, there is no assurance whatever that it will stay down, or that somebody will not have caught a gleam from it on its way to the graveyard.

*Following a student revolt in Budapest in October 1956 that resulted in the formation of a new government headed by Imre Nagy, Soviet tanks entered the city on November 4, crushing Hungary's brief revolution. The emissary is probably Pal Maleter, a general of the revolutionaries, who was arrested by the Soviets while on a mission negotiating Soviet withdrawal from Hungary.

KHRUSHCHEV AND I
(A STUDY IN SIMILARITIES)

9/26/59

UNTIL I HAPPENED TO READ a description of him in the paper recently, I never realized how much Chairman Khrushchev and I are alike. This fellow and myself, it turns out, are like as two peas. The patterns of our lives are almost indistinguishable, one from the other. I suppose the best way to illustrate this striking resemblance is to take up the points of similarity, one by one, as they appear in the news story, which I have here on my desk.

Khrushchev, the story says, is a "devoted family man." Well, now! Could any phrase more perfectly describe me? Since my marriage in 1929, I have spent countless hours with my family and have performed innumerable small acts of devotion, such as shaking down the clinical thermometer and accidentally striking it against the edge of our solid porcelain washbasin. My devotion is too well known to need emphasis. In fact, the phrase that pops into people's heads when they think of me is "devoted family man." Few husbands, either in America or in the Soviet Union, have hung around the house, day in and day out, and never gone anywhere, as consistently as I have and over a longer period of time, and with more devotion. Sometimes it isn't so much devotion as it is simple curiosity—the fun of seeing what's going to happen next in a household like mine. But that's all right, too, and I wouldn't be surprised if some of the Chairman's so-called devotion was simple curiosity. Any husband who loses interest in the drama of family life, as it unfolds, isn't worth his salt.

Khrushchev, the article says, "enjoys walking in the woods with his five grandchildren." Here, I have to admit, there is a difference between us, but it is slight: I have only three grandchildren, and one of them can't walk in the woods, because he was only born on June 24th last and hasn't managed to get onto his feet yet. But he has been making some good tries, and when he does walk, the woods are what he will head for if he is anything like his brother Steven and his sister Martha and, of course, me. We all love the woods. Not even Ed Wynn loves the woods better than my grandchildren and me. We walk in them at every opportunity, stumbling along happily, tripping over windfalls, sniffing valerian, and annoying the jay. We note where the deer has lain under the wild apple, and we watch the red squirrel shucking spruce buds. The hours I have spent walking in the woods with my grandchildren have been happy ones, and I hope Nikita has had such good times in his own queer Russian way, in those strange Russian woods with all the bears. One bright cold morning last winter, I took my grandchildren into the woods through deep snow, to see the place where we were cutting firewood for our kitchen stove (I probably shouldn't tell this, because I imagine Khrushchev's wife has a modern gas or electric stove in her house, and not an old wood-burner, like us Americans). But anyway, Martha fell down seventeen times, and Steven disappeared into a clump of young skunk spruces, and I had all I could do to round up the children and get them safely out of the woods, once they had become separated that way. They're young, that's the main trouble. If anything, they love the woods too well.

The newspaper story says Khrushchev leads a "very busy" life. So do I. I can't quite figure out why I am so busy all the time; it seems silly and it is against my principles. But I know one thing: a man can't keep livestock and sit around all day on his tail. For example, I have just designed and built a cow trap, for taking a Hereford cow by surprise. This job alone has kept me on the go from morning till night for two weeks, as I am only fairly good at constructing things and the trap still has a few bugs in it. Before I became embroiled in building the cow trap, I was busy with two Bantam hens, one of them on ten eggs in an apple box, the other on thirteen eggs in a nail keg. This kept me occupied ("very busy") for three weeks. It was rewarding work, though, and the little hens did the lion's share of it, in the old sweet barn in the still watches of the night. And before that it was haying. And before haying it was baby-sitting—while my daughter-in-law was in the hospital having John. And right in the middle of everything I went to the hospital myself, where, of course, I became busier than ever. Never spent a more active nine days. I don't know how it is in Russia, but the work they cut out for you in an American hospital is almost beyond belief. One night, after an exhausting day with the barium sulphate crowd, I had to sit up till three in the morning editing a brochure that my doctor handed me—something he had written to raise money for the place. Believe me,

I sank down into the covers tired *that* night. Like Khrushchev, I'm just a bundle of activity, sick or well.

Khrushchev's wife, it says here, is a "teacher." My wife happens to be a teacher, too. She doesn't teach school, she teaches writers to remove the slight imperfections that mysteriously creep into American manuscripts, try though the writer will. She has been teaching this for thirty-four years. Laid end to end, the imperfections she has taught writers to remove from manuscripts would reach from Minsk to Coon Rapids. I am well aware that in Russia manuscripts do not have imperfections, but they do in this country, and we just have to make the best of it. At any rate, both Mrs. Khrushchev and my wife are teachers, and that is the main point, showing the uncanny similarity between Khrushchev and me.

Khrushchev, it turns out, has a daughter who is a "biologist." Well, for goodness' sake! *I* have a *step*daughter who is a biologist. She took her Ph.D. at Yale and heads the science department at the Moravian Seminary for Girls. Talk about your two peas! Incidentally, this same stepdaughter has three children, and although they are not technically my grandchildren, nevertheless they go walking in the woods with me, so that brings the woods total to five, roughly speaking, and increases the amazing similarity.

Khrushchev's son is an "engineer," it says. Guess what college my son graduated from! By now you'll think I'm pulling your leg, but it's a fact he graduated from the Massachusetts Institute of Technology. He hasn't launched a rocket yet, but he has launched many a boat, and when I last saw him he held the moon in his hand—or was it a spherical compass?

"The few hours Khrushchev can spare for rest and relaxation he usually spends with his family." There I am again. I hope when Khrushchev, seeking rest and relaxation, lies down on the couch in the bosom of his family, he doesn't find that a dog has got there first and that he is lying on the dog. That's my biggest trouble in relaxing—the damn dog. To him a couch is a finer invention than a satellite, and I tend to agree with him. Anyway, in the hours I can spare for rest, it's family life for me. Once in a great while I sneak down to the shore and mess around in boats, getting away from the family for a little while, but every man does that, I guess. Probably even Khrushchev, devoted family man that he is, goes off by himself once in a great while, to get people out of his hair.

Already you can see how remarkably alike the two of us are, but you haven't heard half of it. During vacations and on Sundays, it says, Khrushchev "goes hunting." That's where I go, too. It doesn't say what Khrushchev hunts, and I won't hazard a guess. As for me, I hunt the croquet ball in the perennial border. Sometimes I hunt the flea. I hunt the pullet egg in the raspberry patch. I hunt the rat. I hunt the hedgehog. I hunt my wife's reading glasses. (They are in the pocket of her housecoat, where any crafty hunter knows they would be.) Nimrods from away back, Khrush and I.

Khrushchev has been an "avid reader since childhood." There I am again. I have read avidly since childhood. Can't remember many of the titles, but I read the books. Not only do I read avidly, I read slowly and painfully, word by word, like a child reading. So my total of books is small compared to most people's total, probably smaller than the Chairman's total. Yet we're both avid readers.

And now listen to this: "Mr. Khrushchev is the friend of scientists, writers, and artists." That is exactly my situation, or predicament. Not all scientists, writers, and artists count me their friend, but I do feel very friendly toward Writer Frank Sullivan, Artist Mary Petty, Scientist Joseph T. Wearn, Pretty Writer Maeve Brennan, Artist Caroline Angell, Young Writer John Updike—the list is much too long to set down on paper. Being the friend of writers, artists, and scientists has its tense moments, but on the whole it has been a good life, and I have no regrets. I think probably it's more fun being a friend of writers and artists in America than in the Soviet Union, because you don't know in advance what they're up to. It's such fun wondering what they're going to say next.

Another point of similarity: Mr. Khrushchev, according to the news story, "devotes a great deal of his attention to American–Soviet relations." So do I. It's what I am doing right this minute. I am trying to use the extraordinary similarity between the Chairman and me to prove that an opportunity exists for improving relations. Once, years ago, I even wrote a book* about the relations between nations. I was a trifle upset at the

*The Wild Flag. (Boston: Houghton, 1946).

time, and the book was rather dreamy and uninformed, but it was good-spirited and it tackled such questions as whether the moon should be represented on the Security Council, and I still think that what I said was essentially sound, although I'm not sure the timing was right. Be that as it may, I'm a devoted advocate of better relations between nations—Khrush and I both. I don't think the nations are going about it the right way, but that's another story.

"No matter how busy Khrushchev is," the article says, "he always finds time to meet Americans and converse with them frankly on contemporary world problems." In this respect, he is the spit and image of me. Take yesterday. I was busy writing and an American walked boldly into the room where I was trying to finish a piece I started more than a year ago and would have finished months ago except for interruptions of one sort and another, and what did I do? I shoved everything aside and talked to this American on contemporary world problems. It turned out he knew almost nothing about them, and I've *never* known much about them, God knows, except what I see with my own eyes, but we kicked it around anyway. I have never been so busy that I wouldn't meet Americans, or they me. Hell, they drive right into my driveway, stop the car, get out, and start talking about contemporary problems even though I've never laid eyes on them before. I don't have the protection Khrushchev has. My dog welcomes any American, day or night, and who am I to let a dog outdo me in simple courtesy?

Mr. Khrushchev, the story goes on, "has a thorough knowledge of agriculture and a concern for the individual worker." Gee whizz, it's me all over again. I have learned so much about agriculture that I have devised a way to water a cow (with calf at side) in the barn cellar without ever going down the stairs. I'm too old to climb down stairs carrying a twelve-quart pail of water. I tie a halter rope to the bail of the pail (I use a clove hitch) and lower the pail through a hatch in the main floor. I do this after dark, when the cow is thirsty and other people aren't around. Only one person ever caught me at it—my granddaughter. She was enchanted. Ellsworth, my cow, knows about the routine, and she and her calf rise to their feet and walk over to the pail, and she drinks, in great long, audible sips, with the light from my flashlight making a sort of spot on cow and pail. Seen from directly above, at a distance of only four or five feet, it is a lovely sight, almost like being in church—the great head and horns, the bail relaxed, the rope slack, the inquisitive little calf attracted by the religious light, wanting to know, and sniffing the edge of the pail timidly. It is, as I say, a lovely, peaceable moment for me, as well as a tribute to my knowledge of agriculture. As for the individual worker whom Khrushchev is concerned about, he is much in my mind, too. His name is Henry.*

Well, that about winds up the list of points of similarity. It is perhaps worth noting that Khrushchev and I are not *wholly* alike—we have our points of difference, too. He weighs 195, I weigh 132. He has lost more hair than I have. I have never struck the moon, even in anger. I have never jammed the air. I have never advocated peace and friendship; my hopes are pinned on law and order, the gradual extension of representative government, the eventual federation of the free, and the end of political chaos caused by the rigidity of sovereignty. I have never said I would bury America, or received a twenty-one-gun salute for having said it. I feel, in fact, that America should not be buried. (I like the *Times* in the morning and the moon at night.) But these are minor differences, easily reconciled by revolution, war, death, or a change of climate. The big thing is that both Khrushchev and I like to walk in the woods with our grandchildren. I wonder if he has noticed how dark the woods have grown lately, the shadows deeper and deeper, the jay silent. I wish the woods were more the way they used to be. I wish they were the way they could be.

*Henry Allen, White's indispensable helper on the Maine farm.

MOON LANDING

THE MOON, it turns out, is a great place for men. One-sixth gravity must be a lot of fun, and when Armstrong and Aldrin* went into their bouncy little dance, like two happy children, it was a moment not only of triumph but of gaiety. The moon, on the other hand, is a poor place for flags. Ours looked stiff and awkward, trying to float on the breeze that does not blow. (There must be a lesson here somewhere.) It is traditional, of course, for explorers to plant the flag, but it struck us, as we watched with awe and admiration and pride, that our two fellows were universal men, not national men, and should have been equipped accordingly. Like every great river and every great sea, the moon belongs to none and belongs to all. It still holds the key to madness, still controls the tides that lap on shores everywhere, still guards the lovers who kiss in every land under no banner but the sky. What a pity that in our moment of triumph we did not forswear the familiar Iwo Jima scene and plant instead a device acceptable to all: a limp white handkerchief, perhaps, symbol of the common cold, which, like the moon, affects us all, unites us all.

---

*During the Apollo 11 mission, Neil Armstrong and Edwin "Buzz" Aldrin took the first steps on the moon July 20, 1969 ("One small step for man, one giant leap for mankind").

7

Body and Mind

HUNGER

4/4/31

YESTERDAY IN THE GRAYBAR BUILDING I bumped into my friend Philip Wedge, looking like the devil. The sight of him gave me a start—he was horribly thin, nothing but skin and bones.

"Hello, Wedge," I said. "Where is the rest of you?"

He smiled a weak smile. "I'm all right."

We chatted for a few moments, and he admitted he had lost almost forty pounds; yet he seemed disinclined to explain. Had it been anybody but Philip Wedge, I would have dropped the subject, but this queer skeleton fascinated me and I finally persuaded him to come along to lunch. At table, we got to the root of the thing quickly enough, for when the waiter appeared Wedge simply shook his head.

"I don't want anything."

"Good Lord," I said, "why not?"

Wedge fixed his eyes on me, the hollow gaze of a death's-head. "Look here," he said, sharply, "you think I'm broke, or sick. It happens I'm neither. I can't eat food, and I'm going to tell you why."

So while I listened he poured it out, this amazing story. I shall set it down as it came from him, but I cannot describe his utter emaciation of body, his moribundity of spirit, as he sat there opposite me, a dying man.

"It wasn't so bad," he began, "while I still had coffee. Up to a few weeks ago I used to get along pretty well on coffee. Practically lived on it. Now even coffee is gone."

"Gone?" I asked.

"Full of rancid oil," said Wedge, drearily. "In its natural state the coffee bean contains a certain amount of oil. This gets rancid, same as any oil." He drew from his pocket an advertise-

105

ment telling about rancid oil in coffee. When I had read it, he folded it and returned it to his pocket.

"I haven't always been this way," he continued. "I used to eat what was set before me. I believe it all started when I learned about marmalade's being made out of bilgewater."

"Out of what?" I gasped.

"Bilgewater. I was only fourteen. A friend of my father's, visiting at our house, told us. The oranges are brought to Scotland from Spain in the holds of ships. During the voyage the oranges float around in the bilge, and when they are unloaded the bilgewater is dumped out with them. The manufacturers find that it gives the marmalade a rich flavor."

"Holy Moses," I murmured. Wedge raised his hand.

"I could never eat marmalade after that. Wouldn't have mattered, of course, but soon other foods began to be taken from me. A year later I learned about wormy pork. Saw an item in the paper. Whole family wiped out, eating underdone pork. Awful death. I haven't had a mouthful since."

I glanced down at my plate and gently pushed it to one side.

"Used to be crazy about cheese," Wedge went on. "Did you ever see the bulletin that the Department of Agriculture issued in regard to mold? If you sniff mold it starts to grow in your lungs, like seaweed. Sometimes takes years but finally gets you. I gave up everything that might be moldy, even bread. One night I was opening a bottle of French vermouth, and the top of the cork was alive with mold. I haven't had a peaceful moment since. Jove, it seems as though every day I learned something awful about food. Ripe olives—every time I opened a newspaper, one or two dinner parties poisoned, people dying like rats. Sometimes it was éclairs. In 1922 I learned about what happens if you eat spinach from a can."

Wedge looked at me steadily.

"The vaguest rumors used to prey on my mind: casual remarks, snatches of overheard conversation. One time I came into a room where a radio was going. A speaker was ending his talk: '. . . or sulphuric acid from dried apricots, or the disintegration of the spleen from eating a poor grade of corn syrup.' That was all I heard. Haven't touched any dried fruit or any syrup since.

"Maybe you recall the track meet some years ago in Madison

Square Garden, when Paavo Nurmi* collapsed. Put his hand to his side, threw back his head, and collapsed. That was veal. Still, even with wormy pork and veal gone, my diet wasn't so bad until I found out about protein poisoning: somebody ate meat and eggs and nuts, and swelled up. I gave up all meat and all eggs, and later all nuts. At meals I began to see not the food that was actually before me—I'd see it in its earlier stages: oysters lying at the mouths of typhoid rivers, oranges impregnated by the citrus fly, gin made from hospital alcohol, watercress in drainage ditches, bottled cherries dipped in aniline dyes, marshmallows made of rotten eggs, parsley vines covered with green caterpillars, grapes sprayed with arsenate of lead. I used to spend hours in my kitchenette testing cans of foodstuffs to see if the cans sat flat. If a can doesn't sit flat, it has an air bubble in it, and its contents kill you after a few hours of agony.

"I grew weaker right along, hardly took a mouthful of anything from day to day. I weigh ninety-five now. All I've had since yesterday morning is a graham cracker. I used to drink quite a lot—alcohol kept me going. Had to quit. Fragmentary bits of gossip I picked up: '. . . lay off the Scotch in the West Forties,' 'The liqueurs contained traces of formaldehyde,' '. . . she died of fusel oil in homemade wine.' I even gave up cigars when I heard how they were made. You know how the ends of cigars are sealed?"

I nodded.

"Life is hell these days. I'm wasting away fast, but it's better than eating things you're scared of. Do you know what happens inside the human stomach when fruit is eaten in combination with any of the root-vegetables such as carrots, turnips . . . ?" Wedge's voice was failing. His eyelids drooped.

I shook my head.

"Enough gas is formed to inflate a balloon the size of . . ."

Wedge swayed in his chair, then slumped down. The poor chap had fainted. When he came to, I held a glass of water to his lips, but he motioned it away.

"Not potable," he murmured. "Reservoirs . . . too low." Then he fainted again. In the sky over Forty-third Street a buzzard wheeled and wheeled on motionless wings.

*Finnish long-distance runner, winner of nine gold medals in the 1920, 1924, and 1928 Olympics.

UP AND DOWN

FEELING FIT AS A FIDDLE, we dropped into the Psychiatric Institute the other afternoon, to pay a small call. Maybe you don't know it, but the Institute has two entrances—one on Riverside Drive, another about a hundred feet above on 168th Street. Anyway, we entered from 168th Street, stepped into the elevator, and asked for the sixth floor. Just as we were bracing ourself for the ascent, the car dropped out from under us, descended a flight or two, the door flew open, and the operator (who by this time we suspected was one of the patients) waited for us to get out.

"Sixth floor," he said, sternly.

We stepped out, gibbering, and it *was* the sixth floor. Luckily we come from hardy stock and can withstand colossal japes like that; but we should think it would be tough on the nervous patients of the Institute, particularly those that are troubled by little men who chase them up airy mountains, down rushy glens.

MY PHYSICAL HANDICAP, HA, HA

6/12/37

SIX MONTHS AGO I began to suffer from dizziness. It is an unhinging of the equilibrium, a condition of the body which gives rise to queer street effects, dreams, and fancies. I will be walking along the street, say, and will take three normal steps in a forward direction; then, as I am about to set my foot down for the fourth step, the pavement moves an inch or two to the right and drops off three-quarters of an inch, and I am not quick enough for it. This results in my jostling somebody on my left, or hitting the corner of the Fred F. French Building a glancing blow. It was fun for a few days, but I have recovered from the first fine ecstasy of dizziness, and am getting bored with it. Once I sidled into a police horse, and he gave me back as good as I gave him.

Although I am sick of my dizziness, I can't say my friends are. They still go into gales of laughter over my infirmity, and if I had lost both legs and travelled in a tiny cart drawn by a span of Baltimore orioles, I don't think I could give them more pleasure. I have consulted doctors, but doctors lose interest in any man who sticks to the same story. At first they were suspicious of my teeth, so I let them have a couple to calm them down. Then they fooled around with some flora they claim grow in the intestines, but they soon learned they were in a blind alley. Several of my friends have tried amateur witchcraft on me, including one lady who insists that my trouble is psychological; she says I stagger through streets because, deep in my heart, I loathe streets. She is, of course, a mad woman. If there's anything I enjoy (or used to), it's messing around the streets.

After listening to friends and doctors, I have drawn my own conclusion about my staggering. I am of the opinion that I have simply lost the knack of walking. Is that so incredible? A biped's ability to get along smoothly on only two legs has always seemed implausible to me. What if I say I've lost the trick? I don't think such an explanation is half so crazy as that I ought to have my tonsils out—which is the most far-fetched idea I ever heard of.

However, I didn't sit down to write about my physical disability; I sat down to write about how I amuse myself now that I am handicapped. At first it was no easy matter. I couldn't work; and while that in itself is amusing, it isn't everything. For a while I had a bad time, but one day, thumbing through a copy of *Hygeia*, I ran onto a list of things to do—a page of suggestions called "Suggested Activities for Persons With Impaired Health or Physical Handicaps," and for the first time I really felt as though I had hold of something.

The list was alphabetical, and apparently had been running as a serial, because in my copy (the April number) the list started with the "J"s and went through the "P"s. I lit a cigarette, snuggled into the couch, where I wouldn't feel dizzy, and began in earnest:

Jail, help families whose father or mother is in

This suggestion, though ingenious, I discarded. I had never helped anybody whose father or mother was in jail even when I was well, and it would be a queer time to start just because I happened to feel bad myself. I continued:

Jam, exhibit for state fair
Journalism, study for

This was getting closer. I ordered currants, raspberries, gooseberries, ten pounds of sugar. They are still around the house, mute reminders of my jam-making days. But I didn't stop with the "J"s, I went on to the "K"s.

Keep watch for the milkwagon horse
Knit, knit, knit, be one of the millions
Kitchen aprons, sell to tourists

I didn't see why I should sell the only kitchen apron in the house to tourists, especially since I contemplated making jam; but it *was* fun knitting and being one of the millions. I did that for two or three days, till I got complained about. In odd moments, I watched for the milk horse, and he for me. Life was indeed straightening out.
Then came the "L"s:

Languages, study by phonograph records and textbooks
Lease your barn for a summer theatre
Leather tooling
Listening ear (Manhattan cocktail at 5 A.M.)

And the "M"s:

Marmosets, breed
Milkwagon horse, keep watch for the
Mineralogy, study on your walks in wood (with hammer along)
Minks, breed
Missing antiques, hunt for
Mothers, adult education for young
Mothers of several small children, watch
Music, study, compose, teach

I let my barn, tooled a little leather, and one morning I arose at five o'clock and mixed myself a Manhattan. It made the day.

Even the marmosets, breeding steadily among themselves, seemed less quarrelsome seen through alcohol's beneficent haze. Streets, and street staggering, began to seem a long way off. I found that a man can occupy himself pleasantly without walking all over town. Quietly, through the long spring evenings, I watched a mother of several young children, and she returned the stare. My minks were sterile but good company. The only "M" that let me down was the mineralogy walks—for me they would have been only another dizzy stagger. And besides, I never carry a hammer. Not after what I've read in the papers.

I'm down to the "N"s now:

Newspapers, sell
Newspapers, send forgotten lines of poem to inquirer in
Night popstands at summer theatre, sell hot coffee or sandwiches
Nurse, have a versatile

There seems to be something for a handicapped man in all these suggestions. The last one practically has my name written on it.

LIFE PHASES

2/20/37

WE ARE NOT SURE we agree with President Roosevelt that seventy is the age when a Supreme Court judge should retire. If we must establish an arbitrary pension age, it should be either fifty or ninety, but not seventy. At seventy, men are just beginning to grow liberal again, after a decade or two of conservatism. Their usefulness to the state is likely to improve after the span of life which the Bible allows them is complete. The men of eighty whom we know are on the whole a more radical, ripsnorting lot than the men of seventy. They hold life cheaply, and hence are able to entertain generous thoughts about the state. It is in his fifty-to-seventy phase that a man pulls in his ears, lashes down his principles, and gets ready for dirty weather. Octogenarians have a more devil-may-care tactic: they are sometimes quite willing to crowd on some sail and see if they can't get a burst of speed out of the old hooker yet.

A man's liberal and conservative phases seem to follow each other in a succession of waves from the time he is born. Children are radicals. Youths are conservatives, with a dash of criminal negligence. Men in their prime are liberals (as long as their digestion keeps pace with their intellect). The middle-aged, except in rare cases, run to shelter: they insure their life, draft a will, accumulate mementos and occasional tables, and hope for security. And then comes old age, which repeats childhood—a time full of humors and sadness, but often full of courage and even prophecy.

GUILTY GUMS

12/17/49

NOW THAT CHILDREN'S TEETH can be protected by adding fluorine to their drinking water, dentists are casting around for some new place to sink their drills. It looks as though they may have found it, too. Last week, Dr. Robert S. Gilbert told his fellow-dentists that a patient's open mouth is a stage on which is enacted the drama of his emotional life. Plenty of people who complain of toothache are just upset, and he (Gilbert) has himself cured a man whose teeth were hurting because of guilt feelings about a dead sister. This is wonderful news, this broadening of the scope of dentistry. We, in our own lifetime, have seen dentistry come a long way. We recall clearly the days when a cavity was a hole that a dentist could feel by poking about with his pry. Then came X-ray, and a cavity was something that the dentist could see on the negative but the patient couldn't, and dentists would drill according to a plotted position on a chart, crashing their way through fine, sturdy old walls of enamel to get to some infinitesimal weakness far within. Now dentists are in search of guilt, not caries, and go rummaging around among the gums for signs of emotional instability. The toothpaste people will undoubtedly follow along—guilt paste, fear paste, and old Doc Lyon's psychosomatipowder.

RADIOGRAPHY

2/24/51

MODERN MEDICINE has led us down many a dead-end street, up many a stagnant backwater, following health's gleam. None of our previous excursions, though, can match last week's trip, which ended in a brand-new radiography room where the operator, a young lady, was unfamiliar with the new, bigger, faster machine and candidly admitted it. It was there, in that fateful chamber, that the old art of healing, long in decline, seemed at last to expire.

Strangely enough, our journey had started with a simple nosebleed the day before. The bleeding persisted, so our doctor suggested that we get the offending blood vessel cauterized. Obediently, we got it cauterized—a simple, early-morning nasal tuneup in the gay East Seventies. The treatment, of course, induced sneezing, and we sneezed steadily and happily while riding downtown to the office. As we stepped from our cab, we were suddenly stricken with an enormous back pain. (In middle life, the human back is spoiling for a technical knockout and will use the flimsiest excuse, even a sneeze, to fall apart.) When our pain failed to subside, we phoned our doctor and reported it, and he ordered us to start upstream again next morning, to be interviewed and photographed. This trip, as it turned out, consumed exactly five hours and wrote a new chapter in ordeal by radiography.

Some temperaments are probably well adapted to the role of guinea pig—to standing or lying in unnatural poses while somebody tries to get the hang of a new camera—but ours is not one of them. Gowned in the classic cotton tie-back frock of the X-ray victim—the frock with the plunging hipline—we exposed our bony structure for countless takes and retakes while the operator tentatively fooled with the new knobs, fought the new adjustments, and shook her pretty head over the new formulae for exposure. The machine, with its baffling wall charts, was obviously too complex for the human mind to grasp, and our sympathy at this point was with the girl. After all, we told ourself, it's no worse than taking a trial spin in a space ship, with Ed Wynn at the controls (and his bright, childish laughter at the takeoff).

An hour passed—with intervals of sitting outside in the hall waiting for plates to be developed. Gradually the idea assailed us that we were absorbing more rays than a Bikini* goat. Our back pain was almost gone—just a memory, really. Our nose showed not a trace of blood. But our condition was bad, and if we had been running the joint we would have placed ourself immediately on the critical list and prescribed massive doses of whiskey.

When the first two series of pictures failed to reveal a human spine, the operator called for help. A new girl showed up, and a conference was held, in which we were invited to join. "What d'ya say we just forget these *new* charts," murmured the consultant, "and use the old one that we always used to use" (the one, we presumed, that went with the other machine—the old, slow, reciprocating job of yesteryear). At this idea the girls brightened perceptibly, and one of them put the matter squarely up to us. "Don't you think," she asked, "that there's nothing like the old *tried* formulas?"

We mustered a tiny smile and nodded, and she disappeared behind her lead wall. "Stop breathing!" she commanded, speaking through the slot in the wall. We stopped breathing. The vast machine, goaded by the old, tried formula, retched

---

*The Bikini Islands in the Pacific were the site of two peacetime atomic bomb tests in July 1946 ("Operation Crossroads").

and wheezed and bored through us. "Breathe!" she cried. But there was no zest for breath any more, no grounds for inhalation, and we walked airily away, trailing the grotesque gown, along the endless corridor, toward the last dressing room.

If any doctor wants us again, he will first have to start up the breathing.

THE COLD

11/10/51

WE ARE AT THIS WRITING IN BED, entertaining our first cold of the 1951–52 virus season. It would greatly satisfy our curiosity to know at precisely what moment the virus gained entrance and took hold—for there must have been such a moment, such a division point. Prior to that moment, we were a whole man; subsequent to it, and until the symptoms appeared, we were the unwitting host to evil and corruption. One wonders about all such tremendous turning points: the moment when a child is conceived, the moment when the tide stops flooding and starts ebbing. We have often wondered at precisely what moment in life our defenses were successfully breached by another, deadlier virus—the point that marked the exact end of youth's high innocence and purity of design, the beginning of compromise, acquiescence, conformity, and the general lassitude of maturity. There must in every person's life (except a few rare ones) have been such a moment. In the case of the cold, the lag between the penetration of the disease and the appearance of the symptoms is a matter of hours; in the case of the other virus, a matter of years.

Statisticians have computed the very great interruptive strength of the common cold in our society, have shown how it slows the wheels of industry. That is only one side to the virus, however. We are such docile creatures, normally, that it takes a virus to jolt us out of life's routine. A couple of days in a fever bed are, in a sense, health-giving; the change in body temperature, the change in pulse rate, and the change of scene have a restorative effect on the system equal to the hell they raise. We heard once of a man who went to bed with a cold one day and never got up again. The seizure was soon over and his health restored, but the adventure of being in bed impressed him deeply and he felt that he had discovered his niche at last.

Medical science understands this paradox of the virus, and virus diseases are now the white hope of cancer research. (It has already been shown that they tend to congregate in cancer cells.) Thermometer in mouth, we await the day of victory, when the common cold, which has long been the butt of our anger, will emerge as the knight that slew the dragon.

CRICKET-IN-THE-EAR

9/13/52

MID-SEPTEMBER, the cricket's festival, is the hardest time of year for a friend of ours who suffers from a ringing in the ears. He tells us that at this season it is almost impossible, walking or riding in the country, to distinguish between the poetry of earth and the racket inside his own head. The sound of insects has become, for him, completely identified with personal deterioration. He doesn't know, and hasn't been able to learn from his doctor, what cricket-in-the-ear signifies, if anything, but he recalls that the Hemingway hero in "Across the River and Into the Trees" was afflicted the same way and only lasted two days—died in the back seat of an automobile after closing the door carefully and well. Our friend can't disabuse himself of the fear that he is just a day or two from dead, and it is really pitiful to see him shut a door, the care he takes.

HOSPITAL VISIT

2/16/57

MODERN MEDICINE IS A WONDERFUL THING, but we doubt whether it ever catches up with modern man, who is way out in front and running strong. One morning at the hospital, the *Times* was delivered to our breakfast table (by a woman tall enough to reach to that dizzy height) and we turned idly to an article on tranquillizers, headed "WARNS OF HEALTH PERIL." Clinicians, the article said, have found some of the effects of the drugs to be Parkinsonism, allergic dermatitis, constipation, diarrhea, jaundice, and depression. We finished our frozen juice and turned to face an entering nurse, who presented us with a tiny paper cup containing a white pill. "Take this," she said, smiling a knowing smile. We bowed and she left. We picked up the pill, examined it closely, and there, sure enough, was the familiar monogram of Miltown. Dutifully we swallowed it, and immediately felt the first symptoms of Parkinson's disease, the first faint flush of yellow jaundice. Then we looked back at the tray and noticed that our morning milk had arrived in a wax-paper carton—the same sort of carton that was in the news some months ago, suspected by scientists of being carcinogenic. Recklessly we poured the milk and raised the glass to our image in the mirror. "Cheers!" we croaked, and fell back onto the pillows, in the last stages of allergic dermatitis.

The curative value of a hospital, for us, is that it keeps us busy. In our normal life in the outside world, we seldom have anything to do from morning till night and we simply wander about, a writer who rarely writes, lonely and at peace, getting through the day cunningly, the way an alcoholic works his way along from drink to drink, cleverly spaced. But once we're in a hospital, the nights and days are crowded with events and accomplishment. Supper is at six, breakfast at nine, which means that for about fifteen hours we subsist in a semistarved condition, like a man in a lifeboat; and when our stomach is empty our mind and heart are full, and we are up and about, doing housework, catching up on correspondence, outwitting the air-conditioning system, taking sleeping pills, reading names on nurses' badges, arranging flowers, picking up after the last tenant, fighting the roller shade that has lost its spring, making plans for death, inventing dodges to circumvent therapy, attaching a string to the bed table to render it accessible to the immobilized patient, flushing undesirable medication down the toilet, prying into the private affairs of the floor nurse, gazing out at the wheeling planets and the lovely arabesques of the Jersey shore. Dawn comes, and an early nurse, to test with her little fingers whether our heart still beats. And then we shave and practice counting to fifteen, so that when they jab us with Sodium Pentothal and ask us to count, we can race them to the knockout. Busyness is really the solution to a man's life, in this cold sunless clime. And a hospital is the place.

THE ICE DANCE

3/23/35

THE WINTER ends on a clear, high note with the fabulous ice extravaganza at the Garden.* Skating, which has a sort of cold purity anyway, has suddenly come to be one of the most exciting expressions—to us the ice dance is potentially a greater thing than the dance. If we were a student of the dance, we'd sell our little shoon and buy ourself a pair of skates; there is a sublimity about skating, cold as a fountain, warm-blooded as love, extra-dimensional, an ecstatic emancipation which Maude Adams hinted at when, trussed up by a wire, she flew across the stage and translated every child's dream. A few skaters have begun to realize what can be done in musical interpretation, have given up acrobatics and grapevines, and

*The Skating Club of New York sponsored a sold-out international ice-skating show March 13, 1935 at Madison Square Garden benefiting Bellevue Hospital Social Relief Service. Vivi-Ann Hulten was the Swedish skater, Louise Bertram and Stewart Reburn the Canadian skaters. Maude Adams was an American actress who played Peter Pan on stage in 1905.

settled down to set their skates to music. We remember Graf-strom, the Swede; he was an inspired dancer, the first we ever saw. The other night Miss Hulten, also of Sweden, gave a beautiful exhibition, and so did a pair from Toronto, dancing to "Isle of Capri." The Garden, in half-darkness, seemed to cohere, faces in shadow, the spotlight trailing the silvery course of the dance—a really thrilling thing to watch. Ice is an odd substance to have at last freed the body in its persistent attempt to catch up with the spirit.

8

Science

MYSTERIES OF LIFE

9/22/28

ABOUT ONCE A YEAR the human soul gets into the papers, when the British scientists convene. Once a year the mystery of life, the riddle of death, are either cleared up or left hanging. The reports of the learned men enthrall us, and there have been moments when we've felt that we were really approaching an understanding of life's secret. We experienced one of those moments the other morning, reading a long article on the chemistry of the cell. Unfortunately, when we finished we happened to glance into our goldfish tank and saw there a new inhabitant. Frisky, our pet snail, had given birth to a tiny son while our back was turned. The baby mollusk was even then hunching along the glassy depths, wiggling his feelers, shaking his whelky head. Nothing about Frisky's appearance or conduct had given us the slightest intimation of the blessed event; and gazing at the little newcomer, we grew very humble, and threw the morning paper away. Life was as mysterious as ever.

SEEING THINGS

THE NEW REPTILE HALL was officially opened a few days ago in the Museum of Natural History and we visited it amidst a group of youngsters who kept crying "Good night!" and their mothers who kept murmuring "Mercy!" The place is like that. It might be called the Conan Doyle Hall, with certain exhibits marked: "Strong Influence of Lewis Carroll." Things out of the dead worlds of Sir Arthur's writings and Mr. Carroll's "Looking Glass" are here but you have to accept the word of eminent scientists that they once lived. Place of honor goes to the dragon lizards which, brought from the Dutch West Indies, lived for a while at the Bronx Zoo. They look like dinosaurs reduced nine-tenths and, in fact, were spotted for dinosaurs by excited travellers who saw them rear up on their hind legs at a distance and gave the Sunday papers an annual feature story for ten years until the Museum went down and caught a few. The largest is nine feet long.

Even taking into account the grimly handsome Sphlenodon, which looks exactly like William Boyd in the last act of "What Price Glory," we like most the group of fat Brazilian horned frogs which have soft velvety black and green heads and must have been cronies of Tweedledum and his brother. Some of the exhibits tie up neatly with literature, such as the Russell's Viper, which has the title rôle in the Sherlock Holmes story, "The Speckled Band," and the tiny mongoose which is the Rikki-tikki-tavi of Kipling's tales. The mongoose is shown snapping its fingers at a King Cobra, which mongooses devote their life to chivvying about and killing, thus becoming, in our opinion, the world's bravest animal.

In one case reposes the world's largest frog, and although right next door is a tiny reptile whose sex life and fighting skill are described minutely, the sign by the world's largest frog frankly says, "Nothing is known of its habits," thus giving us an example of the oddities of scientific research to ponder about the rest of our life. All the snakes are here, including one with no card telling what it is, and the Green Mamba, which is as lovely as a jade necklace and as poisonous as the devil. The snake that interested us most, though, is the Pine Snake, for this is the one the lady snake charmers play with, and it is described as harmless and of very gentle disposition, the worst it ever does being to make a noise like a hot iron plunged into water.

We never go to the Museum but we look up two favorite exhibits of ours. One is the incredible raccoon bear, a cross between those two animals and, we like to believe, a sheer figment of the craftsmanship of the whimsical doctor who said he found one in Tibet. The other is the thirty-six-ton siderite which Peary* brought back from Greenland after two vain tries. The sign tells of the immensity of the task and relates that the mammoth hunk of almost pure iron was finally brought here and given to the museum. But how this was done is left to our imagination, which never fails to be both interested and baffled.

TECHNOLOGICAL PROGRESS

7/13/35

ON A ROCKY ISLAND in the blue sea, shining white, its tall tower naked and beautiful in the sun, a lighthouse stood, abandoned. We passed by in a boat, remembering when the place was full of life, the keeper tending his light and drawing his pay, his wife hanging out flannel drawers to the seabreeze, his children, like Captain January's daughter, roving the island, watching the ships. Now, in the channel, three or four hundred yards off the rocks, is a gas buoy, winking its mechanical warning, supplanting a whole family. To us, an idle mariner on a painted ocean, the empty lighthouse seemed a symbol of all that is going on in the world: new devices putting men and their families out of work. As we passed the forsaken island and stared at the boarded-up windows and thought about the fam-

*Robert Edwin Peary, arctic explorer who reached the North Pole April 6, 1909.

ily applying for relief and the Congress worrying about new taxes to provide the dole, we wondered whether it wouldn't just have been simpler, somehow, for the government never to have bought a gas buoy. Is it really cheaper to support a lighthouse keeper on relief than to support him in his lighthouse? Science, blessing us with gas buoys, is a hard master and perhaps an evil one, giving us steel for flesh, dole for wages, solving every problem save the essential one: what to do about the pride of a former lighthouse-keeper, who doesn't want relief, who wants bread earned by toil, seeing his light shine afar.

Of course, the defenders of scientific progress claim that for every displaced victim of technology, there is a new job opening up—if not in the service industries, or in entertainment, then in the field of invention. Maybe this is true. Certainly there are some queer new jobs that one hears about these days. There is the engineer, for instance, who carved out a niche for himself in the world by devising an apparatus which copes with the problem of the flies which hover by the thousands over the manure beds on mushroom farms. A huge fan sucks the flies across a refrigerating coil, which chills them and drops them, dormant, into large milk cans. The lids are then clamped on the milk cans and the flies are shipped to frog-growers, who chill them again and serve them, with a dash of bitters, to frogs. Maybe some ex-lighthouse-keeper can busy himself, in our brave new world, by thinking up something nifty like that.

GRAVITY

4/3/37

IT SEEMS AS THOUGH NO LAWS, not even fairly old ones, can safely be regarded as unassailable. The force of gravity, which we have always ascribed to the "pull of the earth," was reinterpreted the other day by a scientist who says that when we fall it is not earth pulling us, it is heaven pushing us. This blasts the rock on which we sit. If science can do a rightabout-face on a thing as fundamental as gravity, maybe Newton was a sucker not to have just eaten the apple.

There's one thing about this new gravitational theory, though: it explains the fierce, frenzied noise that big airplanes make, fighting their way through the inhospitable sky. We now know that a plane, roaring through the air, is not straining against the attraction of one friendly earth, but is sneering loudly at the repulsion of innumerable stars.

SILENCE OF THE SPHERES

10/30/48

ASTRONOMY IS NO LONGER a mere matter of gazing at the stars; one must listen to them, too. The Milky Way sends on a frequency of 14.2 megacycles. The other galaxies and the sun maintain a tighter broadcasting schedule than N. B. C. There is, in fact, a sort of cosmic signal always going out to the earth, and the new equipment of our astrophysicists enables them to hear it as plainly as a soap opera. It sounds, in the words of a Harvard listener, "like a combination of gravel falling on the roof and the howling of wolves." If we remember right, the *silence* of the spheres had something to do with the conversion of Pascal: he discovered faith when he became conscious of silence. Little did he know how noisy his world was, how deceptive silence can be (and the nearness of wolves and the steady rain of gravel).

The time in our own life when we came closest to being convinced by silence was one time at sea in a light fall of snow. We heard nothing—no gravel, no wind, no wave, no wolves, no bell buoy. It was convincing and it was beautiful. We are sorry to learn, at this date, that there was nothing to it.

HOT PIPES

3/1/52

WE READ A NEWS STORY the other day telling about the withdrawal of a group of young atomic scientists from the world. When the doors closed behind them, these fellows entered a life as pure and as remote as that of a monk on a mountaintop. Instead of disappearing into puffs of cumulus clouds, they vanished into the swirling mists of secrecy. It gave us quite a turn, secrecy being the slow death of science, purity its most debilitating quality. Science can't possibly serve people well till it belongs openly to all and associates itself with wisdom and sense—those contaminating but healthful influences.

We saw a remarkable example, recently, of an architect's remoteness from the world—as though he had withdrawn to his own private mountaintop. We chanced to pay a visit to a student's dormitory room in an engineering college, to see how things were going. The building was a modern one, and of course the designer must have had access to the vast storehouse of technical knowledge that the institution had assembled through the years, so we expected to find something pretty good in the way of digs—something sensible, if modest. What we found was an immaculate little torture chamber suitable for cremating a cat in. The temperature was 92°. Two large steam-pipes extended from floor to ceiling. These supplied constant heat, day and night. The only way to subdue the hot pipes was to open the window. The only place the bed would fit was under the window. The student admitted, under close questioning, that his living conditions were less than marginal and said he'd already been to the infirmary with a stiff neck caused by extreme exposure. He was not at all disgruntled, however, and was at work on a counter architectural wonder of his own—a system of baffles to carry the cold outside air directly onto the hot pipes, bypassing the bed, confounding the original designer, raising the institution's fuel bill, and investing the room with a Goldbergian quality proper to youth. We looked over his schedule while we were there. One of his courses was something called Heat Engineering. Probably the architect who designed the room took the same course, years ago, and got honors. But it isn't enough that a designer understand Heat Engineering to save humanity, he must have once slept next to a hot pipe.

FRED ON SPACE

11/16/57

WHEN THE NEWS BROKE about the dog in the sky, I went down into the shabby woods below my dump to see if Fred's ghost was walking. Fred* is a dead dachshund of mine. He is restless in death, as he was in life, and I often encounter his

---

*White said of Fred, "Of all the dogs whom I have served I've never known one who understood so much of what I say or held it in such deep contempt." Fred was a main character in several essays: "Bedfellows" and "Death of a Pig" (*Essays*) and "Dog Training" and "A Week in November" (*One Man's Meat*). Fred was a spirited individualist and White continued to admire him long after his death in 1948. The "dog in the sky" Fred and White are discussing in this piece was the first animal launched in a space capsule (the Soviets' Sputnik 2, November 1957).

ghost wandering about in the dingle where his grave is. There are a couple of wild apple trees down there, struggling among hackmatacks to gain light. A grapevine strangles one of these trees in its strong, purple grip. The place is brambly, rank with weeds, and full of graves and the spirits of the departed. Partridges like it, and so do skunks and porcupines and red squirrels, so it is an ideal spot for Fred's ghost. I went down because I felt confused about the Russian satellite and wanted to interview Fred on the subject. He was an objectionable dog, but I learned a lot from him, and on this occasion I felt that his views on outer space would be instructive.

Fred's ghost was there, just as I suspected it might be. The ghost pretended not to notice me as I entered the woods, but that was a characteristic of Fred's—pretending not to notice one's arrival. Fred went to Hell when he died, but his shade is not touchy about it. "I regret nothing," it told me once. The ghost appeared to be smoking a cigar as I bearded him for the interview. The interview follows, as near as I can recapture it from memory:

Q—The Soviet Union, as you probably know, Fred, has launched a second rocket into space. This one contains a female dog. Would you care to comment on this event?

A—Yes. They put the wrong dog in it.

Q—How do you mean?

A—If they wanted to get rid of a dog the hard way, they should have used that thing you have up at the house these days—that black puppy you call Augie. There's the dog for outer space.

Q—Why?

A—Because he's a lightweight. Perfect for floating through space, vomiting as he goes.

Q—Vomiting? You think, then, that nausea sets in when the pull of gravity ceases?

(Fred's lips curled back, revealing a trace of wispy foam. He seemed to be smiling his old knowing smile.)

A—Certainly it does. Can you imagine the conditions inside that capsule? What a contribution to make to the firmament!

Q—As an ex-dog, how do you feel about space in general? Do you think Man will emancipate himself by his experiments with rockets?

A—If you ask me, space has backfired already.

Q—Backfired?

A—Sure. Men think they need more space, so what happens? They put a dog in a strait jacket. No space at all, the poor bitch. I got more space in Hell than this Russian pooch, who is also sick at her stomach. Hell is quite roomy; I like that about it.

Q—The Russian dog is said to be travelling at seventeen thousand eight hundred and forty miles an hour. Do you care to comment on that?

A—Remember the day I found that woodchuck down by the boathouse? Seventeen thousand miles an hour! Don't make me laugh. I was doing a good eighteen if I was moving at all, and I wasn't orbiting, either. Who wants to orbit? You go around the earth once, you've had it.

Q—News accounts from Moscow this morning say the space dog is behaving quietly and happily. Do you believe it?

A—Of course not. There's a contradiction in terms right there. If the bitch was happy, she wouldn't be quiet, she'd be carrying on. The Russians are a bunch of soberpusses; they don't know what clowning means. They ring a bell when it's time for a dog to eat. You never had to ring a bell for me, Buster.

(This was quite true. But I felt that I would learn nothing if Fred's ghost started reminiscing, and I tried hard to keep the interview on the track.)

Q—The Russians picked a laika to occupy the space capsule. Do you think a dachshund would have been a wiser choice?

A—Certainly. But a dachshund has better things to do. When a car drives in the yard, there are four wheels, all of them crying to be smelled. The secrets I used to unlock in the old days when that fish truck drove in! Brother! If a dog is going to unlock any secrets, don't send him into space, let him smell what's going on right at home.

Q—The fame of the Russian dog is based on the fact that it has travelled farther from the earth than any other living creature. Do you feel that this is a good reason for eminence?

A—I don't know about fame. But the way things are shaping up on earth, the farther away anybody can get from it these days, the better.

Q—Dog lovers all over the world are deeply concerned about the use of a dog in space experiments. What is your reaction?

A—Dog lovers are the silliest group of people to be found anywhere. They're even crazier than physicists. You should hear the sessions we have in Hell on the subject of dog lovers! If they ever put a man in one of those capsules for a ride out yonder, I hope it's a dog lover.

(Fred's shade thinned slightly and undulated, as though he was racked with inner mirth.)

Q—This satellite with a dog aboard is a very serious thing for all of us. It may be critical. All sorts of secrets may be unlocked. Do you believe that man at last may learn the secret of the sun?

A—No chance. Men have had hundreds of thousands of years to learn the secret of the sun, which is so simple every dog knows it. A dog knows enough to go lie down in the sun when he feels lazy. Does a man lie down in the sun? No, he blasts a dog off, with instruments to find out his blood pressure. You will note, too, that a dog never makes the mistake of lying in the hot sun right after a heavy meal. A dog lies in the sun early in the day, after a light breakfast, when the muscles need massaging by the gentle heat and the spirit craves the companionship of warmth, when the flies crawl on the warm, painted surfaces and the bugs crawl, and the day settles into its solemn stride, and the little bantam hen steals away into the blackberry bushes. That is the whole secret of the sun—to receive it willingly. What more is there to unlock? I find I miss the sun: Hell's heat is rather unsettling, like air-conditioning. I should have lain around more while I was on earth.

Q—Thank you for your remarks. One more question. Do you feel that humans can adapt to space?

A—My experience with humans, unfortunately, was largely confined to my experience with you. But even that limited association taught me that humans have no capacity for adapting themselves to anything at all. Furthermore, they have no *intention* of adapting themselves. Human beings are motivated by a deeply rooted desire to change their environment and make *it* adapt to them. Men won't adapt to space, space will adapt to men—and that'll be a mess, too. If you ever get to the moon, you will unquestionably begin raising the devil with the moon. Speaking of that, I was up around the house the other evening and I see you are remodelling your back kitchen—knocking a wall out, building new counters with a harder surface, and installing a washing machine instead of those old set tubs. Still at it, eh, Buster? Well, it's been amusing seeing you again.

Q—One more question, please, Fred. The dog in the capsule

has caused great apprehension all over the civilized world. Is this apprehension justified?

A—Yes. The presence anywhere at all of an inquisitive man is cause for alarm. A dog's curiosity is wholesome; it is essentially selfish and purposeful and therefore harmless. It relates to the chase or to some priceless bit of local havoc, like my experiments in your barnyard with the legs of living sheep. A man's curiosity, on the other hand, is untinged with immediate mischief; it is pure and therefore very dangerous. The excuse you men give is that you must continually add to the store of human knowledge—a store that already resembles a supermarket and is beginning to hypnotize the customers. Can you imagine a laika sending up a Russian in order to measure the heartbeat of a man? It's inconceivable. No dog would fritter away his time on earth with such tiresome tricks. A dog's curiosity leads him into pretty country and toward predictable trouble, such as a porcupine quill in the nose. Man's curiosity has led finally to outer space where rabbits are as scarce as gravity. Well, you fellows can have outer space. You may eventually get a quill in the nose from some hedgehog of your own manufacture, but I don't envy you the chase. So long, old Master! Dream your fevered dreams!

9

The Academic Life

NO CRACKPOTS?

9/12/42

WE NOTICED, with some misgivings, that the American Federation of Teachers put out a warning the other day that there would be no "crackpots" admitted to its membership. Only those teachers would be admitted who would be a credit to the Federation and instill in boys and girls an abiding loyalty to the ideals and principles of democracy. But as we understand it, one of the noblest attributes of democracy is that it contains no one who can truthfully say, of two pots, which is the cracked, which is the whole. That is basic. The Federation better welcome all comers, and let pot clink against pot.

Education is such a serious matter, we speak of it with trepidation. We remember, with sober and contrite heart, that our educational system was responsible for (among others) the group of citizens who for two years did everything in their power to prove that the war which was going on did not involve us, that nothing was happening abroad which was of any consequence in our lives, that the earth was not round. Those people—millions of them—were all educated in American schools by non-crackpots. They were brought up on American curricula. They damn near did us in. They are ready again to do us in, as soon as an opening presents itself—which will be immediately after hostilities cease. On the basis of the record, it would seem that we need what crackpots we can muster for education in our new world. We need educators who believe that character is more precious than special knowledge, that vision is not just something arrived at through a well-ground lens, and that a child is the most hopeful (and historically the most neglected) property the Republic boasts.

ACADEMIC FREEDOM

2/26/49

WHEN THE PROFESSORS were dismissed from the University of Washington,* the president remarked that allegiance to the Communist Party unfitted a teacher for the search for truth. The argument, it seemed to us, had a certain merit. To pursue truth, one should not be too deeply entrenched in any hole. It is best to have strong curiosity, weak affiliations. But although it's easy to dismiss a professor or make him sign an affidavit, it is not so easy to dismiss the issue of academic freedom, which persists on campuses as the smell of wintergreen oil persists in the locker rooms. In this land, an ousted professor is not an island entire of itself; his death diminishes us all.

There is no question but that colleges and universities these days are under pressure from alumni and trustees to clean house and to provide dynamic instruction in the American way of life. Some institutions (notably Washington University and Olivet College) have already taken steps, others are uneasily going over their lists. Professors, meanwhile, adjust their neckties a little more conservatively in the morning, qualify their irregular remarks with a bit more care. The head of one small college announced the other day that his institution was through fooling around with fuzzy ideas and was going to buckle down and teach straight Americanism—which, from his description, sounded as simple as the manual of arms. At Cornell, an alumnus recently advocated that the university install a course in "Our Freedoms"—possibly a laudable idea but one that struck us as being full of dynamite. (The trouble here is with the word "our," which is too constricting and which would tend to associate a university with a national philosophy, as when the German universities felt the cold hand of the Ministry of Propaganda.) President Eisenhower† has come out with

---

*Herbert J. Phillips and Joseph Butterworth were dismissed because of membership in the Communist Party; Ralph H. Gundlach, who denied that he was a member, was dismissed for "neglect of duty" and an "ambiguous" relationship to the party. Three other professors who admitted that they were once members of the party but had left it were placed on probation. The University of Washington's president was Raymond B. Allen.

†Dwight D. Eisenhower was president of Columbia University from 1948 to

a more solid suggestion, and has stated firmly that Columbia, while admiring one idea, will examine all ideas. He seems to us to have the best grasp of where the strength of America lies.

We on this magazine believe in the principle of hiring and firing on the basis of fitness, and we have no opinion as to the fitness or unfitness of the fired professors. We also believe that some of the firings in this country in the last eighteen months have resembled a political purge, rather than a dismissal for individual unfitness, and we think this is bad for everybody. Hollywood fired its writers in a block of ten. The University of Washington stood its professors up in a block of six, fired three for political wrongness, retained three on probation. Regardless of the fitness or unfitness of these men for their jobs, this is not good management; it is nervous management and it suggests pressure. Indirectly, it abets Communism by making millions of highly fit Americans a little cautious, a little fearful of having naughty "thoughts," a little fearful of believing differently from the next man, a little worried about associating with a group or party or club.

A healthy university in a healthy democracy is a free society in miniature. The pesky nature of democratic life is that it has no comfortable rigidity; it always hangs by a thread, never quite submits to consolidation or solidification, is always being challenged, always being defended. The seeming insubstantiality of this thread is a matter of concern and worry to persons who naturally would prefer a more robust support for the beloved structure. The thread is particularly worrisome, we think, to men of tidy habits and large affairs, who are accustomed to reinforce themselves at every possible turn and who want to do as much for their alma mater. But they do not always perceive that the elasticity of democracy is its strength—like the web of a spider, which bends but holds. The desire to give the whole thing greater rigidity and a more conventional set of fastenings is almost overwhelming in these times when the strain is great, and it makes professed lovers of liberty propose measures that show little real faith in liberty.

We believe with President Eisenhower that a university can

1952; in 1950 he took a leave of absence from Columbia to serve as Supreme Allied Commander of the North Atlantic Treaty Organization. In 1952 he was elected President of the United States.

best demonstrate freedom by not closing its doors to antithetical ideas. We believe that teachers should be fired not in blocks of three for political wrongness but in blocks of one for unfitness. A campus is unique. It is above and beyond government. It is on the highest plane of life. Those who live there know the smell of good air, and they always take pains to spell truth with a small "t." This is its secret strength and its contribution to the web of freedom; this is why the reading room of a college library is the very temple of democracy.

SELECTING SCHOOL BOOKS

10/8/49

THE BOARD OF EDUCATION has twenty-three criteria for selecting textbooks, library books, and magazines for use in the public schools. We learned this by reading a fourteen-page pamphlet published by the Board explaining how it makes its choice. One criterion is: "Is it [the book or magazine] free from subject matter that tends to irreverence for things held sacred?" Another criterion is: "Are both sides of controversial issues presented with fairness?" Another: "Is it free from objectionable slang expressions which will interfere with the building of good language habits?"

These three criteria by themselves are enough to keep a lot of good books from the schools. Irreverence for things held sacred has started many a writer on his way, and will again. An author so little moved by a controversy that he can present both sides fairly is not likely to burn any holes in the paper. We think the way for school children to get both sides of a controversy is to read several books on the subject, not one. In other words, we think the Board should strive for a well-balanced library, not a well-balanced book. The greatest books are heavily slanted, by the nature of greatness.

As for "the building of good language habits," we have gone

carefully through the pamphlet to see what habits, if any, the Board itself has formed. They appear to be the usual ones—the habit of untidiness, the habit of ambiguity, the habit of saying everything the hard way. The clumsy phrase, the impenetrable sentence, the cliché, the misspelled word. The Board has, we gather, no strong convictions about the use of the serial comma, no grip on "that" and "which," no opinion about whether a textbook is a "text book," a "text-book," or a "textbook." (The score at the end of the fourteenth was "text book" 5, "text-book" 11, "textbook" 5.) It sees nothing comical, or challenging, in the sentence "Materials should be provided for boys and girls who vary greatly in attitudes, abilities, interests, and mental age." It sees no need for transposition in "Phrases should not be split in captions under pictures." It sees no bugs in "The number of lines should be most conducive to readability." And you should excuse the expression "bugs"—a slang word, interfering with the building of good language habits.

We still have high hopes of getting *The New Yorker* accepted in the schools, but our hopes are less high than they were when we picked up the pamphlet. We're bucking some stiff criteria— criteria that are, shall we say, time-tested?

THE LIVING LANGUAGE

2/23/57

BETWEEN BERGEN EVANS on the television and a man named Ellsworth Barnard* in the papers, English usage has become hot news; the rhetorical world is almost as tense, at the moment, as the Middle East. Professor Barnard wrote a piece

*Evans hosted "The Last Word" on CBS; Bernard's article in the New York *Times*, "Good Grammar Ain't Good Usage" (17 Jan. 1957: VI, 20), brought a number of responses from readers, some of which the *Times* printed (10 Feb. 1957: VI, 15).

in the *Times* a while back thumbing his nose at grammar and advising teachers to quit boring their pupils with the problem of "who" and "whom." The Professor was immediately ambushed by grammarians and purists in great numbers, and their shafts came zinging from behind every tree in the forest. Meanwhile, Bergen Evans and his panelists were stirring up the masses and egging them on to err. Mr. Evans believes that the language is a living thing and we mustn't strangle it by slavish attention to the rules. Winston Cigarettes, of course, backs him to the hilt, as a cigarette should.* Our prediction is that along Madison Avenue bad grammar, as an attention-getter, will soon be as popular as mutilation—which started with an eye patch and rapidly spread to arms and legs. As Arthur Godfrey sometimes remarks, in one of his contemplative moments, "Who's sponsoring this mess?"

The New Yorker has been up to its ears in English usage for thirty-two years (thirty-two years this very week) and has tried to dwell harmoniously in the weird, turbulent region between a handful of sober grammarians, who live in, and an army of high-spirited writers, who live wherever they can get a foothold. The writer of this paragraph, who also lives in, has seen with his own eyes the nasty chop that is kicked up when the tide of established usage runs against the winds of creation. We have seen heavy, cluttery pieces, with faults clinging to them like barnacles, lifted out of their trouble by the accurate fire of the grammarian (who has the instincts of a machine gunner), and we have also seen the blush removed from a peach by the same fellow's shaving it with an electric razor in the hope of drawing blood. Somewhere in the middle of this mess lies editorial peace and goodness, but, like we say, it's a weird world. Through the turmoil and the whirling waters we have reached a couple of opinions of our own about the language. One is that a schoolchild should be taught grammar—for the same reason that a medical student should study anatomy. Having learned about the exciting mysteries of an English sentence, the child can then go forth and speak and write any damn way he pleases. We knew a countryman once who spoke with wonderful vigor and charm, but ungrammatically. In him the absence

*Winston's advertising jingle was "Winston tastes good like a cigarette should."

of grammar made little difference, because his speech was full of juice. But when a dullard speaks in a slovenly way, his speech suffers not merely from dullness but from ignorance, and his whole life, in a sense, suffers—though he may not feel pain.

The living language is like a cowpath: it is the creation of the cows themselves, who, having created it, follow it or depart from it according to their whims or their needs. From daily use, the path undergoes change. A cow is under no obligation to stay in the narrow path she helped make, following the contour of the land, but she often profits by staying with it and she would be handicapped if she didn't know where it was and where it led to. Children obviously do not depend for communication on a knowledge of grammar; they rely on their ear, mostly, which is sharp and quick. But we have yet to see the child who hasn't profited from coming face to face with a relative pronoun at an early age, and from reading books, which follow the paths of centuries.

10

Business

DOG EAT DOG

4/1/33

MOST IMPERATIVE OF RECENT MISSIVES was a letter from *Forbes*, reminding us that we are not a bluebird. "You are not a bluebird," the letter said, gruffly, and then added, "you are a business man." There was a kind of finality about this news, and we read on. "Business is a hard, cold-blooded game today. Survival of the fittest. Dog eat dog. Produce or get out. A hundred men are after your job." If *Forbes* only knew it, goading of this sort is the wrong treatment for us. We are not, as they say, a bluebird. Nobody who reads the *Nation* regularly, as we do, can retain his amateur bluebird standing. As for business, we agree that it is a hard, cold-blooded game. Survival of the fittest. Dog eat dog. The fact that about eighty-five per cent of the dogs have recently been eaten by the other dogs perhaps explains what long ago we noticed about business: that it had a strong smell of boloney. If dog continues to eat dog, there will be only one dog left, and he will be sick to his stomach.

STRIKES

8/6/27

AS WE RODE COMFORTABLY in the subway on the day set
for the transit strike, the thought came to us that strikes are not
what they used to be. We mourn the old days when workers
would quit their jobs in a spontaneous burst of rebelliousness
and high blood-pressure. Lately, strikes have been produced in
the calm manner of musical comedies, with advance announcements of the cast, date of opening, and photographs of the
strike-breakers learning their duties from the smiling, expect-
ant strikers. The police are notified in advance that riots will
begin at 2:30, the same as any matinée. No wonder labor is
disgruntled; it's as bad as community singing.

PREDATORY

3/19/27

AS PERNICIOUS A PIECE OF chicanery as was ever perpe-
trated is the inspired work of one H. W. Miller, who gave up
his seat on the Stock Exchange recently, and since then has
been devoting his time to calling upon friends during office
hours, seemingly for no particular reason. He shows up unan-
nounced, relaxes in a chair, talks half an hour about curiously
dull subjects, makes it clear that he is in no hurry, and finally
makes a vague exit without giving any reason for having
dropped in. This has left his friends weak, irritable, and bewil-
dered.

It now turns out that the merry stock merchant, finding
himself relieved of work, deliberately armed himself with a
sheaf of inanities, stale jokes, and platitudes, and set forth to
avenge himself heartily for all the time he had been unneces-

sarily interrupted during business for the past ten years.

"I am going to do this for two weeks," he said when cornered, "and then I'm going to the country."

This, in our judgment, has something of the fine deliberateness of the bored ex-aviator who bought a Ford when the war was over, installed an airplane engine and a very loud horn, took aboard some ballast, and went abroad in the land insultingly showing his dust to every Lincoln and Stutz from here to Yosemite. That is the actual case, although we don't know the man's name. We do know that he occupied himself pleasantly that way for more than a year, hiding down lanes and waiting for his prey.

WHAT EVERY ADULT SHOULD KNOW

12/31/27

INSURANCE SALESMEN HAVE ALWAYS BEEN glamorous in our eyes, because they go to places we wouldn't dare go and face odds that would make us quail. While we were lunching with one of these dare-devils last week (he had been in our psychology class at college) he unexpectedly confessed all. He told us that the reason it is possible to make what seem to be impossible sales is that the average man secretly believes he can argue the hide off any salesman, and likes to hear himself try. Once he starts arguing, he hangs himself.

After listening to our friend's disclosures, we are in a position to reveal the cardinal principle for insulating oneself against insurance. It is: always make the wrong answer to the salesman's questions, which are all scientifically designed to bring forth the answer Yes. Your salvation lies in saying No. He will, of course, expect you to take the soundness and the general worthiness of the idea of insurance for granted. This never comes into question. Then he will start off very candidly with some such disarming question as this:

"Now, Mr. Fish, as you know I have come to see you about insurance. I assume, sir, that a man of your business integrity has already made provision against unforeseen circumstances, *haven't you*?" (You say Yes.) "Just as a matter of sound business sense you have created an estate for the protection of your wife, *haven't you*?" (You say Yes.) "Furthermore, I assume that you wish your son Roger to enjoy the educational advantages in life that he deserves, *don't you*?" (Another Yes.)

Well, if you say Yes to all these questions you are a goner because he has a whole string of others calling for affirmative answers which lead inevitably to the execution of a policy. The only safe answer, as we said, is No. If you say No he will still go on trying to sell you insurance but he will be too stunned and dazed to accomplish anything.

A good variation is to say, when the salesman refers to your wife: "I left my wife last week." When he speaks of your son, who will soon be ready for college, bite your lips and say that unfortunately your marriage was childless.

Our friend also informs us that in this business they no longer use the term "to sign" a thing; they say: "to write your name." The word "sign" has come to have a sinister tone. Don't let this trick fool you—writing your name is just as binding.

TADPOLES AND TELEPHONES

6/2/28

THERE WAS A LARGE BOWL of tadpoles in the window of the Telephone Building as we came wandering along, lonely as a cloud. We stopped of course—we stop for anything in windows, particularly tadpoles. A sign said: THE TADPOLE REMINDS US. It told how the unfortunate creature, gloomily metamorphic, is forced to rise at intervals to the surface of the water in order to breathe; and it compared his fate to that of the unfortunate business man who has no telephone on his desk and has to rise and leave his work whenever there is a call. It was a fine and a beautiful little object lesson, and we stood enthralled for fifteen minutes, hoping to verify the truth of this neat biological phenomenon, brooding on its neat analogy. The tadpoles, however, seemed not to rise: they rested lazily on the bottom. After ten minutes of waiting we began to shift uneasily from one foot to the other. Still no tadpoles rose to the surface. Could the Telephone Company be wrong? The truth finally seeped into our consciousness: the tadpoles had sensibly *given up* rising to the surface, wise little frogs! We departed, vowing never to answer the phone again.

TRUTH-IN-ADVERTISING

7/11/36

THE TRUTH-IN-ADVERTISING movement has just celebrated its silver jubilee, and everybody laughed when it stepped up to the piano. Advertising is almost the only profession which has spent twenty-five years worrying about its own good character. Most types of enterprise never give truth a second thought, but advertising people are not like that: they keep truth in front of them all the time, brooding dreamily about it while writing the long, long drama of mouth hygiene. They worry so furiously about truth, one suspects they read each other's copy. All this is confusing to the consumer, who has a double responsibility toward advertising, being obliged to read it and keep up with it and buy products on the strength of it, and at the same time sympathize with the advertiser's devotion to truth.

In our opinion, nobody has done justice, artistically, to advertising. It is patently America's major contribution to present-day culture; yet the only books, analytical or critical, we have seen on the subject have been either textbooks, which are dull and special, or books debunking advertising, which are ill-tempered, humorless, and out-of-date before they get into print. The key to the advertising heart (and none of the writers on the subject seems to have grasped this) is this very search for elusive truth, the kind of search that took Byrd to the South Pole even though he knew there was nothing there, the kind of search which after twenty-five years still takes its pilgrims to Boston to a meeting of the Advertising Federation of America, there to rededicate themselves to the principles of the Baltimore convention of 1931. It is this feeling for truth which sets up a local irritation in the breasts of those who have given themselves to the fantasia of depilatories and emollients. They know that the hair must be removed from ladies' arms and men's jowls, yet in the pain of literary composition they find themselves kin to Edgar Allan Poe and Arthur Guy Empey. They are obliged to express an idea on paper, and this takes them into the world of literary creation, artistic jealousy, and truth.

The consumer, if left to his own devices, would no more expect truth in advertising than he would expect honesty in parenthood; after all, it is reasonable to suppose that a manufacturer is biassed about his own product, in the same way that a parent is over-appreciative of his own child. "Advertising," said Mrs. William Brown Meloney at the silver jubilee of truth, "must be the herald of the new and greater world into which we are entering." And one suddenly gets a picture of the devotees exhausted by their zeal, entering into the new and greater world by getting a lift from a nationally advertised cigarette.

Advertisers are the interpreters of our dreams—Joseph interpreting for Pharoah. Like the movies, they infect the routine futility of our days with purposeful adventure. Their weapons are our weaknesses: fear, ambition, illness, pride, selfishness, desire, ignorance. And these weapons must be kept bright as a sword. We rise to eat a breakfast cereal which will give us strength for the tasks of the day; we vanquish the excesses of the night with an alkaline fizz; we cleanse our gums, stifle our bad odors, adorn our diseased bodies, and go forth to conquer—

cheered on with a thousand slogans, devices, lucubrations. What folly for our leaders to meet in Boston in quest of an unwonted truth! We live by fiction. By fiction alone can Man get through the day.

RAVISHED LIPS

4/10/37

WE DO NOT PROFESS TO understand the philosophy of merchandising, but we are willing to go on studying it, just as we have for many years. On the radio we heard a voice say that Angelus lipstick kept lips "ravishing yet virginal." It seems to us highly important to examine this apparent contradiction and to find out where the manufacturer really stands on the question, what his desires and hopes are for the girls who use his product. Does he want them to be ravished, or does he want them to remain virgins? If his desire is that they look ravishing, yet remain untarnished, then what are his feelings, if any, toward the males for whose benefit the cosmetic is applied and whose lot it is to be attracted yet repelled? We think the public has a right to inquire into these things, and be instructed. It is possible that a manufacturer of lipstick has no genuine interest in the potentials of his product. It is also possible that we men, faced with women who are equipped to be both maid and wanton, are deliberately being taken for a sleigh ride.

Bourjois, the scent-maker, points out that romance doesn't just happen: it is won by wearing a perfume called Evening in Paris. And there is the daring new odeur, Gabilla's Sinful Soul, exotic and naughty. One would say that ladies are now enabled to ask, in the language of the odeur, for love licit or illicit, for enduring fidelity or for the wanton tweak. Let us hope that the ladies, with their fragrances, are not embarrassed by a too great confidence in the New York male's sense of smell, debauched as it is by blowing dust, burned motor fuels, and desiccating office heat. How can the ladies tell, anyway, what smells are associated with romance in a gentleman's subconscious? For one is the torpid, alkaline smell of the Interborough; for another, the pure prickle of new linen unfolded by hands suddenly adored; for another, the drying of wet wool before a great fire. Perhaps Elizabeth Arden is wisest—she wants the ladies to smell like a rolling Kentucky landscape, which really takes in quite a lot.

WHAT? THEY DON'T WORK?

7/3/43

THE PAPERS CARRIED only the most modest account of the Federal Trade Commission's complaint against Carter's Little Liver Pills; to wit, that they had no therapeutic effect on the liver. We don't understand the complacency with which the nation received this news, threatening, as it does, to affect millions of lives and organs. From the early days of medicine men and snake oil, the sluggish liver has been an inseparable part of the American dream—the sluggish liver, the healing pill. Our mountains and plains, our cities and villages, were conquered and built by men who had sluggish livers and the means of curing them. The famous little pills travelled the uncharted alimentary canal by the untold billions, and their fame shone forth from the sides of barns and warehouses from one end to the other of this vast and bilious empire. Suddenly we are informed, in one blinding sentence of our government's charge, that not one pill ever reached its destination, not one ever made contact with the human liver, and that the whole thing has been a magnificent delusion. It was as though we had heard one morning that Broadway had in reality never made contact with Forty-second Street, or that Niagara Falls had no actuality but was a mere fiction of lovers. We fail to see why the

Times didn't give the story what it was worth—an eight-column head on the first page: CHARGE CARTER'S PILLS MISSED VITAL ORGAN—130,000,000 PEOPLE REPORTED STILL SLUGGISH.

If the Federal Trade Commission's charges are proved, the early advertising man who first had the Carter's Little Liver Pills account should certainly receive some sort of Congressional decoration for his unique contribution to American hokum. He should be posthumously awarded the coveted ribbon of the Order of the Purple Phrase.

STOCK MARKET ZIGZAGS

3/26/55

WE DON'T FULLY SUBSCRIBE to the bald statement that confidence in this country's economy can be lost in a day. There are tangible assets that are not easily wiped out—the soil, the climate, the industrial vigor, the immense spirit of a people who won freedom through revolutionary zeal and are still willing to work at it. And there are intangibles that give the economy fertility and vitality. The stock market, which is a sort of horse track without the horses, does not deserve its wide reputation as a barometer. It sometimes sows the hurricane, instead of reporting the breeze. It is naturally flighty, because traders are noncreative people who rely for their security on the creativeness of others and who are therefore uneasy. Winchell* mentions a stock by name and a rainbow appears in the sky over Wall Street. But what the market does symbolize, in its nervous way, is the health-giving flexibility of capitalism—the trait that keeps our economy delicately balanced but that makes it a far better servant of the people than the state-driven

*Walter Winchell, news commentator.

155

economies that have hardly any elasticity at all. The other day, in San Diego, the American economy even adjusted to springtime: work was halted on a seven-million-dollar building project to give a dove time to hatch her eggs. Our confidence in a society that observes this sentimental ritual and practices this fiscal folly cannot be toppled in a day. To talk of peace is not enough; we must hatch the egg of the dove.

SPLIT PERSONALITIES

2/19/55

IN THIS AGE OF TELEVISION, this day of the spoken word and the fleeting image, we find ourself taking satisfaction in the printed word, which has a natural durability. Whenever we watch TV, we are impressed by two things: its effectiveness and its evanescence. It glides by and is lost. The printed word sticks around—you can walk into any library thirty years later, and there (for what it may be worth) it is.

The most puzzling thing about TV is the steady advance of the sponsor across the line that has always separated news from promotion, entertainment from merchandising. The advertiser has assumed the role of originator, and the performer has gradually been eased into the role of peddler. This is evident everywhere. The voices of radio and television are the voices of quick-change artists; they move rapidly from selling to telling and back to selling again. They are losing their sharpness because they have divided their allegiance. In 1925, when *The New Yorker* was born, an artist was an artist, a writer was a writer, a newsman was a newsman, an actor was an actor. Today, every one of these people has developed a split personality and is hawking something besides his talent. A newscaster appears on the screen, and for a moment you don't know whether he has tidings about some offshore islands or tidings about an automobile's rear end. Usually he has both. A girl breaks into song, and for a moment you can't quite pin down the source of her lyrical passion. It could be love, it could be something that comes in a jar. Conscious or unconscious, there is an attempt to blur the line that the press has fought to hold. The line would have disappeared long since were the human voice capable of sounding the same in both its roles, but it isn't. When a man speaks words he has been paid to utter, praises something he gets money for praising, his voice invariably gives him away; it simply lacks the accents that reinforce a voice when it is expressing something that comes straight from head or heart. It seems odd to us that commerce should aspire to violate the line, blend the two voices. Yet it does. If the line were to disappear, if the voices should become indistinguishable, the show would be over.

MARKET WATCHERS

12/18/54

ON OUR WAY TO WORK in the morning, we sometimes pass one of those temples where men sit meditating with their hats on, watching ticker reports projected on a screen. We stopped for a moment the other morning to kibitz: through the window we watched the watchers at their watching. The ticker was bringing news of cloudy conditions in the Middle West; rain was expected within forty-eight hours and might have an effect on winter wheat. The watchers, some of whom looked as though they were merely taking refuge indoors from a rain of their own making, absorbed this piece of information solemnly. One man, nursing a cigar, closed his eyes as he tried to conjure up the significance of distant rain on distant wheat. What a strange little band of tardy pioneers they seemed, sifting the wind that failed to touch their cheeks as it blew across prairies they would never see! How sad they looked, these early-morning waifs—no parents, no homes, only a lighted screen on which prices rose and fell amid tidings of great gain!

11

Curiosities and Inventions

HOTSPUR THE SWIFT

3/16/29

TO TELL YOU WHAT make of car Hotspur is, would be to make General Motors insanely jealous. That I must not do. Suffice it to say that Hotspur is a small car, whose leather seats smell. Even the rumble-seat smells, although it is right out in the open.

"Do the seats smell that way just while they are new," I asked the salesman, "or will they always smell that way?"

"You won't notice it after the first five hundred miles," he replied.

"I think my friends will, though," I said.

It's four weeks since I drove Hotspur out of the agency, his windshield plastered with printed directions, his nickel head-lights catching the last gleam of the twilight, his gas swashing around audibly in the gas tank, his right front fender grazing a lady on the sidewalk. They have been four ecstatic weeks. I have obeyed the rules which I found on the windshield, have religiously kept Hotspur down under thirty-five miles an hour, and now my purgatory nears an end, and I will soon be able to open him up to his full forty. The smell still lingers, and even on an open road, brisking right along, I can shut my eyes, inhale, and imagine I am seated in the lobby of a second-rate hotel.

My friends twit me about this smell, just as I expected they would. At first I was sensitive about it and was at the mercy of my joking passengers, but now I forestall their remarks. The moment a guest enters my automobile I turn immediately to him with my nose in the air and inquire: "Have you been around a stable, by any chance?" or: "Have you, do you suppose, something on the bottom of your shoe?" This unsettles the guest and usually he has a miserable time the entire trip.

Hotspur has other traits which my friends have found amusing, but it's surprising how quickly one builds up a defence against jests. Time was when almost anybody could have annoyed me by referring to a certain strange vibrant sound that occurs in Hotspur when he attains a middling speed. It is a noise which comes over him just at twenty-eight miles an hour—it hits him suddenly, and reminds me of the pleasant sound that wagons make when, from afar, you hear them crossing a wooden bridge in the country. When my friends mention the noise, I explain that it is a "harmonic," a sympathetic overtone that can occur only at a certain speed; with this as my theme I go on at some length, telling about musical harmonics and how, when you play a note on the piano, the octave will also vibrate, and I recite, too, instances of church windows being broken by organ notes, and other interesting phenomena of sympathetic vibration, until my friends soon become so absorbed in my discourse that they forget Hotspur's extraordinary unquiet. (Either that or they get out of the car altogether and beat their way home across country.)

So far, the rumble-seat has been used only by women and children. Opinions have differed about it. For the most part, the children have enjoyed it—welcoming, as children do, the terrible exposure in midwinter, the possibility of pneumonia and release from school, the sense of utter helplessness and bounce. The only lady who ever ventured into the rumble skinned her right knee getting in and her left knee getting out, thus preserving a kind of rough symmetry through it all. A day or two later I happened to be asking her to marry me, and mentioned that if she were my wife she could always ride in the rumble. "And open up all the old wounds?" she said, sadly.

She was a lovely person. I will always remember her. I will remember how she turned to me with a heroic little smile on her lips and said:

"The seat would be more comfortable if you wouldn't keep so many empty boxes and crates in there."

"But there aren't any empty boxes and crates in there," I replied, astounded.

"No, I suppose not," she continued, thoughtfully, "and yet that's the impression one gets, somehow."

A month has worked great changes in Hotspur's appearance. His nickel trimmings, that once blinded me with their early

radiance, have toned down to the color and sheen of old candy-
wrappers. His fenders, at first richly ebon, are now a pale pavement blue. In spirit, though, he is the same car. Lately it has
seemed to me that he senses the approach of spring, for sometimes, setting forth with him on one of those clear mornings
that bleed the heart with the prick of distant and unmistakable
crocuses, I have felt a little earthly shiver run through his
frame, and he has leapt ahead with an urgency more than
mechanical, an internal expansion not unlike my own.

BUY A BATTLESHIP?

11/30/29

WE ONCE SERIOUSLY CONSIDERED purchasing the Leviathan* when it was on sale. Somehow we never went through
with it. Now we see by the papers that the government is going
to sell three obsolete cruisers at public auction. One of these
would suit our needs even better than the Leviathan. We suspect it would be a lot of fun to own a battleship, be it ever so
obsolete. It would bolster our ego. How pleasant to overhear
young ladies whispering: "Not the Mr. Tilley who has the battleship?" Pleasant, and advantageous socially. It would be
pleasant, too, to make use of our ship in connection with the
sporadic activities of the regular Navy. We would like to come
on a sham battle on a foggy day and sneak in with *our* cruiser
to participate, first on one side then on the other, annoying
admirals, confusing the issue. It may not be too late. About how
much would a battleship be?

*German ocean liner (originally "Vaterland") that was turned into an Allied
troop transport during World War I, then into a transatlantic passenger liner. It was
scrapped in 1937.

ANIMAL VOICES

2/8/30

WHEN THE NOON WHISTLE BLOWS in Bronx Zoo, it starts the wolves howling. They point their noses high, their breath curls upward on the cold air, and they give tongue in the primeval forests of their cage. Movie people have been trying to record this performance in sound pictures, but without any luck—the wolves refuse to howl into a microphone. It's one of the little city problems that haven't been solved yet.

Animals are rather hard to take in sound pictures, Dr. Ditmars, the snake man, tells us. He has been making sound records of their voices for synchronization with his own moving pictures, and has recorded the sounds of most of the animals in the Park. Lions are disappointing—they sound like a cow, no majesty, only vaguely sad. Metro-Goldwyn-Mayer made a sound record, for its trademark lion, but gave it up, it sounded so feeble and un-metro-goldwyn-mayer. Camels are difficult, and better results are obtained by having a man make a noise like a camel than by taking the camel's voice itself. Strangely enough, one of the best sound artists is the rattlesnake—the sound record of a rattler is perfect. Dr. Ditmars experimented with a wooden rattle in front of the microphone, but could get nothing as good as the real thing. The hiss of the cobra is also rather nice.

A major difficulty is getting the animal to make any sound at all, animals having a penchant for absolute silence. There are different ways of stimulating them. To make a monkey scream with horror, you show it a live snake. To make it chatter with glee, you show it a banana. Tree toads won't perform until you begin sawing up a piece of bronze with a hacksaw—and that spoils the record. Dr. Ditmars wanted to make a katydid record and found that the only way he could induce the katydids to make their monotonous music was by placing other katydids on the outside of his studio, so that his subjects could hear the low distant sound of their love-making. This required a lot of katydids, and necessitated a trip to Wurtsborough Mountain in Jersey, where katydids can be captured at night in the scrub oaks on the mountainside.

According to Dr. Ditmars, the cleanest and most satisfactory way to record animal sounds is to stay away from the animals altogether, and summon a man named Phil Dwyer, who will make any noise you ask for, and who doesn't require any stimulus such as bananas or distant love-making. This Mr. Dwyer was the camel in a fine camel picture made by one of the movie companies. It would have been a great success as a topical picture except that in making up the film they put the camel voice (a mournful and very loud braying noise) on a kangaroo record. The result was surprising, zoölogically, but the braying kangaroo appeared in two Broadway houses before the film company discovered its mistake. Natural history note: kangaroos do not make any noise.

THEN AND NOW

12/9/33

WE RAN ACROSS A 1908 Schwartz catalogue in the course of the week, and it was a lot of fun to compare it with the 1933 catalogue. Fundamentally, toys don't change as much as we imagine. In the current catalogue, for example, you read about a submarine "that dives and rises just like real ones." This seems like ultra-modernity till you turn to the 1908 list and find the same submarine, for slightly less money. The same is true of a diver—a little man who goes to the bottom. Schwartz has one today for $1.50. You could have had a nice five-inch diver in 1908 for forty cents. There was a swimming doll in 1908, identical with today's swimming doll except for her bathing suit, which had a long skirt. There was a very good fireboat in 1908, which threw a stream of water, and a very good cow which gave milk. The 1933 catalogue speaks of a doll that "breathes," but that idea isn't new, either. There used to be a doll that drank milk and wet its pants, and there still is. Farm sets haven't changed; and 1908 was full of jigsaw puzzles, bagatelle, and steam launches. Anchor blocks, those memorable little stone building blocks whose yellow arches, blue turrets, and red cubes formed the framework of our own childhood, are still going strong today; and to our notion nothing has come along which can touch them, in either beauty or practical possibilities.

Toys have, of course, been de-luxed up considerably. Take the Irish Mail, a standard juvenile vehicle even in this scooter age. In 1908, evidences of effeteness were already apparent in the Irish Mail: a model came out called the Fairy Auto Car, which we remember very well because it had a clutch. Equipped with "cushion tires," it sold for $13.50. Today, Schwartz sells a de-luxe Mail, equipped with Goodyear pneumatic balloon tires, electric lights and horn, and front-wheel drive, for $38. The 1933 express wagon has streamlined wheel housings, like a pursuit plane, and one of the 1933 toy coupés is radio-equipped—that is, it gives forth music, like a taxicab. Locomotives on the modern electric railways give forth a chugging noise.

The toy that seems to have gone completely by the board is the tricycle, and by tricycle we don't mean velocipede. We mean the tricycle your sister had, with the two big rear wheels and the one little front wheel and the sway-back frame which gave it its ladylike appearance. The 1908 catalogue featured tricycles, but you never see one today. It took little girls many years to discover that the tricycle was a mechanically inefficient device requiring four times the steam to make it go that it ought to, but they finally found out.

Toys now are sanitary, de-luxe, and faithful miniatures; and a good many of life's little hazards have been eliminated for today's batch of youngsters. We are thinking particularly of the motorboat which goes a hundred and fifty feet, "then turns around and comes back." Maybe we are crazy, but for us the rich charm of a mechanical boat used to be the delicious problem of retrieving it from mid-pond.

FITTING IN

6/9/34

THE COMPLAINT ONE OF OUR FRIENDS makes about modern steel furniture, modern glass houses, modern red bars, and modern streamlined trains and cars is that all these *objets modernes,* while adequate and amusing in themselves, tend to make the people who use them look dated. It is an honest criticism. The human race has done nothing much about changing its own appearance to conform to the form and texture of its appurtenances. Our professors of eugenics have dodged the whole issue. At the Chicago Fair, the noticeable thing about the circular houses of tomorrow was not how funny the houses looked but how funny the people looked in them. Must the next generation be as structurally inefficient, as architecturally inappropriate, as the present? Babies even at this late date are born with ears that stick out and catch the wind; the back of their head fails to come to a long sharp point. It often seems to us that the only people who really fit into the modern picture are certain department-store dummies and occasionally a pattern figure in a fashion magazine. The rest of us definitely don't belong.

SOOTHING THE CHICKENS

5/15/37

THE IMPERSONAL, disjointed sound which radio in large doses makes immunizes the listener. We happen to know one set-owner who has found a practical use for this curious property. He is a Massachusetts poultry farmer who goes in for large-scale egg-raising. He discovered that if his hens were disturbed by a sudden noise in the night, egg production fell off sharply next day. So now he keeps a radio going quietly night and day among his hens, immunizing them against the virus of sound. It works perfectly. Let a door squeak on its hinges; the hens accept it as a sound effect. Somehow it gives us a secret, deep pleasure to know that a dramatized news broadcast, aimed to unnerve the rest of us, is definitely reassuring to a lot of sleepy fowl, dreaming of hawks and weasels in a henhouse far away.

THE OLD AND THE NEW

6/19/37

IN AN EXCURSION along U. S. Highway 1 last weekend, we noted two interesting building operations. One was a theatre being built in the shape of a barn. The other was a restaurant being built in the shape of a diner. It is amusing to see these American forms, which were the result of vicissitudes, being perpetuated after the need is over. Heredity is a strong factor, even in architecture. Necessity first mothered invention. Now invention has some little ones of her own, and they look just like grandma.

REVOLVING DOORS

4/1/44

SOMEBODY HAS PATENTED a revolving door equipped with an electric eye to start it going at "the right moment." In our opinion there is no "right moment" for a door to begin revolving; almost always it's an unhappy compromise between two opposing factions, one trying to get into the building, the other trying to get out. The "right moment" never arrives, although we have seen neurotics hanging around the outskirts hopefully waiting for it. A revolving door is simply an ingenious trap which most people have learned to spring without getting killed. What a revolving door needs is not an electric eye but a steel grabhook to help hesitant ladies and a centrifugal governor to foil the ambitions of human dynamos. An electric eye for a revolving door would need to be fitted with bifocals, because one person's right moment is another person's Dunkirk.*

PERILS OF THE SEA

10/7/44

OWNERS OF SMALL BOATS know that yachting on Long Island Sound has its perilous moments—the sudden squall, the untried guest, the parted halyard, the accidental jibe, the overshot mooring, the eagle-eyed audience on the clubhouse porch. It has its terrible overheated days, too, when the sail mildews because nobody is there to dry it, afternoons when the wind dies and the tide runs foul at the harbor mouth. Having come safely through a summer of trials and dangers afloat, a lady we

---

*Over 300,000 Allied troops were evacuated from France at this seaport in May 1940. France surrendered to Germany in June 1940.

know, captain of an eighteen-foot sailboat, sat down the other evening in the lee of her radio to refresh her memory by reading over the insurance policy she had blithely taken out last spring. For twenty-seven dollars the company had watched over her all season and would continue to watch until the policy expired. "Touching the adventures and perils," she read, "which we, the Assurers, are contented to bear, and do take upon us, they are of the seas, men-of-war, fire, enemies, pirates, rovers, assailing thieves, jettisons, letters of mart and countermart, reprisals, takings at sea, arrests, restraints and detainments of kings, princes, and people, of what nation, condition, or quality soever, barratry of the Master and Mariners, and of all other like perils, losses, and misfortunes that have or shall come to the hurt, detriment, or damage of said yacht or any part thereof." Well, it had been quite a summer. The detainment of a prince, she decided, must have been the day she took that Rye man for a sail and his right arm became unmanageable.

MAKING DO

8/11/45

A FEMALE FRIEND of ours recently moved into a small apartment so full of defects as to be really quite charming. One rather obvious feature was that the place lacked kitchen shelves. After watching the pitiful and on the whole rather frightening preparations her husband made for remedying this defect (he went out and bought some twenty-penny spikes and a bottle of New England rum), our friend decided she would manage *without* kitchen shelves. She got looking around the apartment and observed that the bookshelves in the living room had four or five inches of space behind the books. Quieting her husband, she arranged her supply of canned goods neatly. For extra convenience, she alphabetized everything. Asparagus is behind Sherwood Anderson, cherries behind Conrad, peaches behind Proust. She is as happy as a child about all this.

GET A HANDLE ON IT

3/13/48

TOO OFTEN WHEN YOU LIFT SOMETHING, your hand clutches an unsuitable shape. Seize any teapot, tennis racket, or oxyacetylene blowpipe, and what have you got? A plain handle. Your own marvellously curved digits are wrapped around an unmolded surface, stresses and strains all wrong, and the tea (or oxyacetylene gas) nothing but an awkward struggle. Happily, this state of affairs is about to end. A man named Thomas Lamb has invented a handle consistent with America's destiny, a handle to fit the hand. Soon you will be lifting something—a coal shovel, a machete—and your cunning digits will enfold the new Lamb Wedge-Lock Handle, designed to meet the human grasp as intimately as an ice skater's tights meet a cold leg.

We attended the unveiling of the Lamb handle last week in a small, white, odorless Prest-Glass room in the Museum of Modern Art. The Modern has a rather dreadful knack of giving an oversoul to a ripsaw and imbuing the future with undigested beauty. The blood pounded in our temples as we stared at a diagram of a gorilla's paw and heard the bells of St. Thomas next door, scattering "Lead, Kindly Light" into Fifty-third Street. As far into the future as we could see, there were only perfect handles. Man, the sign said, has achieved dominance through brain and hand, but his hand is still wrapped around the most outrageous old surfaces—plain old suitcase handles, plain old canoe paddles, plain old telephone receivers. No shape to anything the hand slips around unless you want to count a woman's waist. Fitted with the new Lamb Wedge-Lock Handle, your stewpot, your golf club, your castrating knife will take on new meaning. Fatigue and strain noticeably reduced.

We can report that the Lamb looks like any other handle except that it is grooved to take thumb and forefinger and is a bit thicker in some places than in others. It looks like a handle that has softened in the hot weather, been used, and then hardened again in the cold. The Modern always does things up brown, and there was a wall with projecting Wedge-Lock handles, where you could *push* with a Wedge-Lock handle, *pull* with a Wedge-Lock handle, and *twist* with a Wedge-Lock handle. People gravely pushed, pulled, twisted. The handles soon grew sweaty and gave us a queer feeling of the New Sweat. When your hand is around a Lamb, it feels almost too good—a little too pat, you might say. Also, it gives a slight trapped sensation, as when you grasp a bowling ball.

The handle is in production and you will soon be meeting up with it if you are the sort of person that ever takes hold of anything. We found, on trial, that the handle has one disadvantage: unless you seize it in the right place, you're out of the groove and might as well have hold of the wrong end of a gimlet. We strongly recommend, though, that the Brooklyn Dodgers look into it and try a Lamb Wedge-Lock bat handle. If the claims mean anything, it ought to add a hundred feet to any clean drive. Might mean the pennant.

We rode home, after the unveiling, in a crosstown bus, wedged in and hanging fast to an old, unmolded metal strap. Our palm resented every inch of the journey. Hardly anyone in the bus seemed truly happy.

HAND THROTTLE

THIS TOWN IS FULL of persons who sleep fitfully on expensive innerspring mattresses that have been stiffened (or decontaminated) by expensive plywood bedboards, thus giving the sleepers' spines a solid support. These same bewitched persons, who paid through the nose for one slice of modernity only to discover that they had to go back and buy another slice to take the curse off it—these same persons, having brought their beds up to date with a bedboard, may now bring their automobiles up to date with a gadget called a Hande-Feed Finger Tip Gas Control. A mail-order firm in St. Louis is advertising it. It is installed in fifteen minutes. It costs $5.95. The manufacturer claims that it will enable you to relax while you drive—no toe on the accelerator. And if you are an old, old man, it may occur to you that what you are buying as an extra for your modern car is simply the hand throttle that used to be standard equipment on all cars in the days before streamlining set in. These are gay times. A man pays three thousand dollars for a new car, and then shells out an additional $5.95 for a hand throttle. Still, it's a hopeful sign. If auto-gadget makers are beginning to dig into the past for new ideas, maybe they'll come up with a lot of things. We may yet be able to buy special mail-order fenders that permit a car to be parked without the help of radar, and a special mail-order driver's seat that affords the pilot a view of the thirty feet of road immediately ahead of his front bumper.

TAKING IT WITH YOU

10/16/48

IN A RECENT ISSUE OF *The New Yorker,* an advertisement of Oshkosh luggage mentioned that prices ranged "from $25 to $5,000." It seemed like a sweet range, so we wrote Oshkosh and asked which unit they were holding for five thousand dollars. We got back a nice letter saying that it is a special trunk made of alligators and goats. It has thirty-two hangers. Bottom slats are hickory. Covering is alligator. Hardware is triple gold-plated. Lining is imported goatskin, color of Dubonnet. Oshkosh didn't say where the goatskins are from, but we assume they're from Greece, from the original Raymond Duncan milking herd. The trunk enjoys the following equipment, and so would you if you owned the trunk: gold-plated rib-rod trolley, electric iron, ironing board, tilting shoe boxes, corduroy laundry bag, silk curtains, built-in radio with self-charging battery, and a small bar. Every rivet is gold-plated, and the best thing of all is that the trunk has twelve ball-bearing roller casters. "A child can push it around." Oshkosh introduced this child rather suddenly and we didn't catch the little fellow's name, but we can see him at his deadly work—pushing the trunk around and around the room in Shepheard's Hotel while the trunk's radio blares the latest news of inflation in America and the child's father tries to overtake the trunk's bar so that he can pour himself a drink and the child's mother stands in the vortex wondering whether they hadn't better try to sell the trunk to a Cairo dentist for the gold there is in it.

TELEVISION

12/4/48

LIKE RADIO, television hangs on the questionable theory that whatever happens anywhere should be sensed everywhere. If everyone is going to be able to see everything, in the long run all sights may lose whatever rarity value they once possessed, and it may well turn out that people, being able to see and hear practically everything, will be specially interested in almost nothing. Already you can detect the first faint signs of this apathy. Already manufacturers are trying to anticipate it, by providing the public with combination sets that offer a triple threat: radio, record playing, and television—all three to be turned on at once, we presume.

Television, when it gets going, will almost certainly pick up and throw into one's home scenes it didn't reckon on when it set up its camera. There have already been examples of this. In London not long ago, a television broadcaster was giving his impressions of the zoo when a big lizard bit him on the finger. The technicians in charge of the broadcast, delighted at this turn of events, kept their camera trained on the spurting blood. Thus what had begun as a man's impression of an animal ended as an animal's impression of a man, and a few drops of private blood gained general currency and became a great pool of public blood, and the world immediately contained more persons who had seen a lizard bite a man.

AIR-CONDITIONED FIRES

9/12/53

AS YOU APPROACH the taproom of the Holland House Ta-
verne, in Radio City, pressing forward through the small, air-
conditioned American foyer toward the distant Dutch retreat,
you pass a fireplace in which an electric fire burns cheerfully
in a coal grate. Somehow this combination of fire and ice, of
heat and chill, of winterproofing in the midst of summerproof-
ing, brings to a head the American Way in a single interior. It
is an architectural banana split, a perfect case of the debauchery of design. A menu printed almost entirely in Dutch adds
a fillip to a completely American occasion of lunatic splendor
and comfort. There is something so wonderfully insatiable
about this culture of ours. The other day, as we paused in front
of the Holland House fire a moment to recover from the ninety-
five-degree heat of the streets and to wait for a friend, we
reached in our pocket and found there a letter from an engineering firm in Chicago telling us of a device for cutting king-
size cigarettes in half. ("Stop cigarette waste. Save 25 cents a
day. Combination case and cutter cuts king-size cigarettes in
half—for 40 quick, always fresh smokes.") Probably the man
who thought up the idea of adding a cubit to the stature of a
cigarette believed he had hit on something that was for the
ages. It seems doubtful whether he envisioned that in a few
short years somebody would come up with the revolutionary
idea of cutting the longer cigarette down to size. ("Smoke the
half you throw away!") At any rate, we wished we had a cutter.
We would have liked to spend a languorous afternoon there by
the glowing coals in the air-conditioned room, nursing a bottle
of Heineken's beer and slowly slicing cigarettes and allowing
them to fall onto the ashless hearth of the heat-free fire.

BRANDY KEGS

PLENTY OF STORES sell dog supplies—rubber bones, baskets, vitamins, leashes—but Abercrombie & Fitch doesn't stop there. For the past few days Abercrombie has displayed in one of its windows a brandy keg for a St. Bernard's collar. This object, so nicely made, so brilliantly unlikely, holds a curious fascination for us, a man who has been lost in the snows of Forty-fifth Street these many years and whom no dog has suc-cored. We stand and gaze at it every time we pass, admiring its brass bindings and its strap of well-dressed leather. Only a store with a lot of guts would try to pay a high midtown rent by selling brandy kegs for St. Bernards. Of course, New York is a town of eight million inhabitants, many of them buying fools, but even so whole hours must slip by without anybody's dropping in to pick up a keg for a St. Bernard. Another thing that impresses us is the size of the keg. Its girth is about that of a dachshund puppy, and we would say that its capacity is very close to a quart. That's a lot of brandy for a half-frozen man to take aboard—and the least a snowbound man can do if a dog shows up with a drink is drink it.

When Churchill* retired the other day, we felt like sending him something—some gift in appreciation of his having once saved our life. Perhaps a St. Bernard, complete with brandy, would be the perfect present—a dog that would shuffle along at his side as he strolls the grounds of Chartwell, a sort of four-legged hip flask, keeping him supplied with his favorite comfort in the frightening blizzard of old age. We shall have to think about it, though; it's not the sort of project a person should rush into, however much it might stimulate Abercrom-bie, however deep our sense of gratitude to this great man.

---

*Winston Churchill, Prime Minister of Great Britain 1940–45.

GRANDFATHER CLOCKS

2/23/57

ON TV THE OTHER MORNING we heard the old song about the grandfather's clock and how it "stopped short, never to go again, when the old man died." It's a ghostly tale, all right, and we don't intend to challenge its authenticity. We do know one thing about a grandfather's clock, though, from close association: even when you take the weights off, thus depriving it of its source of strength, the clock doesn't stop short. The last time we removed the weights from ours, the clock kept going for ten minutes, from sheer force of habit, or of character, or both, plus the disinclination of all things, animate or inanimate, to let go of life. We were greatly impressed by this extra ten minutes of timekeeping by a clock that had had its jugular cut—more ghostly, in a way, than if we ourself had died and the clock had stopped short. This clock belonged originally to an ancestor of our wife's, who had it built (of cherry) to furnish a house in Stockbridge, Massachusetts, about a hundred and sixty years ago. It still keeps perfect time. In our house, instead of setting the clock by the radio, we set the radio by the clock. (How's that for a ghostly tale?)

12

Christmas Spirit

MIDNIGHT MASS

12/26/36

EVERYONE HAS ONE CHRISTMAS he remembers above all others, one blindingly beautiful occasion. Ours is a Christmas Eve, during calf love, when we made the (for us) adventurous pilgrimage to a midnight Mass in a Catholic church. Church-going in our family had always been in the honest gloom of a Protestant Sunday morning, and we must hasten to explain that the purpose of this clandestine night expedition was far from religious; we simply had reason to suspect that if we visited that church at that hour, we would catch a glimpse of our beloved. Snow began to fall at sundown, and fell quietly all evening. The snow, the lateness of the hour, the elaborate mysteries of the Mass (we had never seen the inside of a cathedral before), together with the steady burning vision of the back of Her neck whom we adored, and then the coming out into the snow alone afterward, with the street lamps veiled in white: this indeed was a holy time.

WOOLWORTH MADONNA

12/26/36

SHOPPING IN WOOLWORTH'S, in the turbulent days, we saw a little boy put his hand inquiringly on a ten-cent Christ child, part of a crèche. "What is this?" he asked his mother, who had him by the hand. "C'mon, c'mon," replied the harassed woman, "you don't want that!" She dragged him grimly away—a Woolworth Madonna, her mind dark with gift-thoughts, following a star of her own devising.

RELATIVE PRONOUNS

12/25/48

WE HAD A SCROOGE in our office a few minutes ago, a tall, parched man,* beefing about Christmas and threatening to disembowel anyone who mentioned the word. He said his work had suffered and his life been made unbearable by the demands and conventions of the season. He said he hated wise men, whether from the East or from the West, hated red ribbon, angels, Scotch Tape, greeting cards depicting the Adoration, mincemeat, dripping candles, distant and near relatives, fir balsam, silent nights, boy sopranos, shopping lists with check marks against some of the items, and the whole yuletide stratagem, not to mention the low-lying cloud of unwritten thank-you letters hanging just above the horizon. He was in a savage state. Before he left the office, though, we saw him transfigured, just as Scrooge was transfigured. The difference was that whereas Scrooge was softened by visions, our visitor was soft-

*Harold Ross, editor of *The New Yorker* from its founding in 1925 to his death in 1951.

182

ened by the sight of a small book standing on our desk—a copy of Fowler's "Modern English Usage."

"Greatest collection of essays and opinions ever assembled between covers," he shouted, "including a truly masterful study of *that* and *which.* "

He seized the book and began thumbing through it for favorite passages, slowly stuffing a couple of small gift-wrapped parcels into the pocket of his greatcoat.

"Listen to this," he said in a triumphant voice. " 'Avoidance of the obvious is very well, provided that it is not itself obvious, but, if it is, all is spoilt.' Isn't that beautiful?"

We agreed that it was a sound and valuable sentiment, perfectly expressed. He then began a sermon on *that* and *which*, taking as his text certain paragraphs from Fowler, and warming rapidly to his theme.

"Listen to this: 'If writers would agree to regard *that* as the defining relative pronoun, and *which* as the non-defining, there would be much gain both in lucidity and in ease. Some there are who follow this principle now; but it would be idle to pretend that it is the practice either of most or of the best writers.' "

"It was the practice of St. Matthew," we put in hastily. "Or at any rate he practiced it in one of the most moving sentences ever constructed: 'And, lo, the star, which they saw in the east, went before them, till it came and stood over where the young child was.' You've got to admit that the *which* in that sentence is where it ought to be, as well as every other word. Did you ever read a more satisfactory sentence than that in your life?"

"It's good," said our friend, cheerfully. "It's good because there isn't a ten-dollar word in the whole thing. And Fowler has it pegged, too. Wait a minute. Here. 'What is to be deprecated is the notion that one can improve one's style by using stylish words.' See what I mean about Fowler? But let's get back to *that* and *which*. That's the business that really fascinates me. Fowler devotes eight pages to it. I got so excited once I had the pages photostatted. Listen to this: 'We find in fact that the antecedent of *that* is often personal.' Now, that's very instructive."

"Very," we said. "And if you want an example, take Matthew 2:1: '. . . there came wise men from the east to Jerusalem, saying, Where is he that is born King of the Jews?' Imagine how that simple clause could get loused up if someone wanted to change *that* to *who*!"

"Exactly," he said. "That's what I mean about Fowler. What was the sentence again about the star? Say it again."

We repeated, "And, lo, the star, which they saw in the east, went before them, till it came and stood over where the young child was."

"You see?" he said, happily. "This is the greatest damn book ever written." And he left our office transfigured, a man in excellent spirits. Seeing him go off merry as a grig, we realized that Christmas is where the heart is. For some it is in a roll of red ribbon, for some in the eyes of a young child. For our visitor, we saw clearly, Christmas was in a relative pronoun. Wherever it is, it is quite a day.

HOLIDAY GREETINGS

12/20/52

FROM THIS HIGH MIDTOWN HALL, undecked with boughs, unfortified with mistletoe, we send forth our tinselled greetings as of old, to friends, to readers, to strangers of many conditions in many places. Merry Christmas to uncertified accountants, to tellers who have made a mistake in addition, to girls who have made a mistake in judgment, to grounded airline passengers, and to all those who can't eat clams! We greet with particular warmth people who wake and smell smoke. To captains of river boats on snowy mornings we send an answering toot at this holiday time. Merry Christmas to intellectuals and other despised minorities! Merry Christmas to the musicians of Muzak and men whose shoes don't fit! Greetings of the season to unemployed actors and the blacklisted everywhere who suffer for sins uncommitted; a holly thorn in the thumb of compilers of lists! Greetings to wives who can't find their glasses and to poets who can't find their rhymes! Merry Christmas to the unloved, the misunderstood, the overweight. Joy to the authors of books whose titles begin with the word "How" (as though they knew)! Greetings to people with a ringing in their ears; greetings to growers of gourds, to shearers of sheep, and to makers of change in the lonely underground booths! Merry Christmas to old men asleep in libraries! Merry Christmas to people who can't stay in the same room with a cat! We greet, too, the boarders in boarding houses on 25 December, the duennas in Central Park in fair weather and foul, and young lovers who got nothing in the mail. Merry Christmas to people who plant trees in city streets; merry Christmas to people who save prairie chickens from extinction! Greetings of a purely mechanical sort to machines that think—plus a sprig of artificial holly. Joyous Yule to Cadillac owners whose conduct is unworthy of their car! Merry Christmas to the defeated, the forgotten, the inept; joy to all dandiprats and bunglers! We send, most particularly and most hopefully, our greetings and our prayers to soldiers and guardsmen on land and sea and in the air—the young men doing the hardest things at the hardest time of life. To all such, Merry Christmas, blessings, and good luck! We greet the Secretaries-designate, the President-elect: Merry Christmas to our new leaders, peace on earth, goodwill, and good management! Merry Christmas to couples unhappy in doorways! Merry Christmas to all who think they're in love but aren't sure! Greetings to people waiting for trains that will take them in the wrong direction, to people doing up a bundle and the string is too short, to children with sleds and no snow! We greet ministers who can't think of a moral, gagmen who can't think of a joke. Greetings, too, to the inhabitants of other planets; see you soon! And last, we greet all skaters on small natural ponds at the edge of woods toward the end of afternoon. Merry Christmas, skaters! Ring, steel! Grow red, sky! Die down, wind! Merry Christmas to all and to all a good morrow!

FEED THE BIRDS!

12/26/53

AT CHRISTMAS ONE SHOULD think about birth—an easy task for us, since we have just returned from a pilgrimage to see a newborn child.* Instead of following a star, we simply followed directions given us by the child's parents; took the ten-o'clock train, and found the infant in Boston, where it lay behind glass in a hospital. No shepherds were abiding there, but there was a nurse in a mask attending, and the glory of the Lord shone round about—a child seen through a glass clearly. Like all very new infants, this one appeared to be clothed in innocence and wisdom, probably more of each than he will ever attain again in his life. In the conventional manner, we brought gifts—a flowering plant, a bottle of wine. Then we went out to the Public Gardens to see Mary and Jesus on the island in the lake, a pale-blue Madonna and Child, with ducks circling around. A Boston lady in a shabby coat fed pigeons and sparrows near us where we sat, and she was soon joined by another lady, in a fur cape, who also had crumbs to offer. A squirrel, who seemed well acquainted with the visitors, waited his chance and leapt astride the cape. The feeding went on for a while: a scene of serenity, good will, and competence, each bird being known individually, the more timid ones being given special treatment. When the second lady arose and departed, she sent a little cry of farewell to her friend. "Goodbye for now!" she said, her voice rising. "Meantime, feed the birds!" This simple, bright warning, hurled against the terrible dark dome of the modern sky of anxiety and trouble, had a gentle, lunatic sound that has since echoed in our ear. It made us aware of our own need to send out at this season some general cry of good will to friends. We hope that another year will see the world of men and birds grow steadier, the free spirit stronger under its afflictive load; we hope the insane hatred of nation for nation will yield to the promise of a fertile world that is ready to be good to all when each is just to the other; we pray for the lifting of

*White's grandson Steven White.

curtains, so that the dimly discernible feeling of community among peoples may shine with a clearer light. We send best wishes for a bright Christmas and for the coming of man's humanity to man. Meantime, feed the birds!

REMEMBRANCE IS SUFFICIENT

12/25/54

IT IS NOT EASY to select the few words each year that shall serve as a Christmas greeting to our readers, wherever (like Mrs. Calabash) they are. While engaged in making the selection, we study the typewriter keys with the gravity you sometimes see in the faces of greeting-card buyers in stationery stores—faces taut with a special anguish (a sailor searching for a valentine message commensurate with his desire, a girl hunting for the right phrase to repair a broken friendship), as though all of life, all of love, must suddenly be captured on a small piece of decorative paper and consigned to the mails. This morning early, when we passed the angels in Rockefeller Center, we wished we could simply borrow a trumpet from one of them and blow our best wishes to the world in a single loud blast, instead of coming to the office and picking around among the confused shapes of a keyboard. But then, a few minutes later, gazing at the Dutch candy house in the window of KLM, we were reminded that everyone constructs a Christmas of his own, in his fashion, in sugar-candy form if need be, and that the quest for beauty, piety, simplicity, and merriment takes almost as many forms as there are celebrants, certainly too many to be covered by one note on a borrowed horn.

No one ever weeps for joy—we have this on good authority. We have it on the authority of a professor at the School of Medicine of the University of Rochester. (EXPERT DEEMS JOY NO CAUSE OF TEARS—*The Times.*) But it is true that at Christmas (season of joy, season of joy-to-the world), tears are not unknown, or even infrequent: many find themselves greatly moved by small events—by minor miracles of home or school or church, by a snatch of music, by a drift of paper snow across a TV screen. It is, of course, not joy but beauty that is responsible for this mild phenomenon: the unexpected gift of sadness—of some bright thing unresolved, of some formless wish unattained and unattainable. Since most of the common satisfactions of Christmas are available at the stores, and for a price, we wish our readers the pleasures that are unpurchasable, the satisfactions unpredictable, the nourishment of tears (if at all convenient).

There is one member of our household who never has to grope for words as we are groping now. She is our Aunt Caroline and she is ninety-two. She has observed all her ninety-two Christmases in good health and excellent spirits, and she is in good health and spirits now. Being so old, she goes back to a more leisurely period, and when she speaks, she speaks with a precision and a refinement rare in this undisciplined century. There is nothing stiff-backed about the furnishings of her mind, but it is her nature to sit erect, to stand erect, and to speak an upright kind of English that is always graceful and exact. A few weeks ago, she said something so close to the theme of Christmas that we shall quote it here. We were sitting with her at lunch in the country, and we apologized for not having taken her for a motor ride that morning to see once again the bright colors in the changing woods. "Why, my dear," she said without hesitating, "remembrance is sufficient of the beauty we have seen."

The sentence startled us—as though a bird had flown into the room. Perhaps her statement, so casually spoken yet so poetical, is a useful clue to the grownups' strange Christmas, the Christmas that often seems so baffling at first, and then so rewarding. At any rate, it suggests the beauty that surrounds the day, the sufficiency of remembrance, the nostalgia that is the source of tears. We are in perfect agreement with the professor at this joyous season; men weep for beauty, for things remembered, for the partridge in the pear tree—the one that their true love brought them and that somehow got mislaid. So we send our greetings to all who laugh or weep or dance or sing, our love to children, our cheers to their embattled parents. To any for whom by some mischance the magical moment fails in reenactment, we give Aunt Caroline's resolute words: Remembrance is sufficient of the beauty we have seen.

13

New York

INTERVIEW WITH A SPARROW

4/9/27

YOU HAVE NOTICED, if you go about much with your eyes on the ground, that English sparrows are resident here in great numbers; they are aperch beneath your bench in the Park, they are rather in the way when you are bringing up alongside the curb in crowded streets, they are in evidence generally. At this season the sparrows are particularly conspicuous because they are in love—and love addles any creature and makes him noisy.

As yet the onset of Spring is largely gossip among the sparrows. Any noon, in Madison Square, you may see one pick up a straw in his beak, put on an air of great business, twisting his head and glancing at the sky. Nothing comes of it. He hops three or four hops, and drops both the straw and the incident.

But it is a sign. Why these birds deliberately endure the hardships of life in town when the wide, fruitful country is theirs for the asking, is a matter of some moment. To content myself on this point I stopped a sparrow recently at the Seventy-second Street entrance of the Park and put the question bluntly.

"Take the matter of food alone," I suggested. "Certainly the rural districts offer inducements."

"That," he replied, "is a common misconception. New York is deceiving. Look at that bench—unpainted, shoddy—and beneath it a drab array of discarded sacks, candy wrappers, and gum labels. But do you (I suppose you don't) know that thirty-five per cent of all peanuts purchased go uneaten and fall to the ground? They are rich in proteins and carbohydrates.

"Crackerjack is also largely spilled. Every Runkel's chocolate wrapper contains important fragments. Only a small part of the oats fed horses at noon is eaten by the horses, because nosebags are difficult to manage and the horse ends by tossing the bag high in the air and spilling the contents. I merely mention these as typical."

The sparrow paused long enough to look into a refuse can.

"Why should I endure the rather stuffy existence in a farmyard," he continued, "when I can reside near a bear's den in a Zoo? Not only is the bear fed out of all proportions to his requirements, leaving me a full crop, but I am also in a position to meet the people, and see them, moreover, in a poor light.

"A man is at his worst when he is standing in front of a bear's den: he tries to appear contemplative and succeeds only in appearing silly, for he knows nothing about bears or he wouldn't be there." I nodded.

"Here in town I can get everything that the country offers, plus the drama, books, the museums, the stimulus of interesting contacts. I took space on a ledge of the Metropolitan two years ago; it afforded an extraordinary outlook on Greek statuary, and influenced my viewpoint. Do you see?"

"But isn't it crowded here in town?" I asked.

"Living conditions are bad, I admit," he replied. "The few trees extant are oversubscribed. But one gets along. There is a certain freedom from restraint. I can go any night to Bryant Park, for example, and slip in among the hundreds of birds which roost in the small tree overlooking the newsstand. It is a rowdy bunch (characteristic of Sixth Avenue) but no questions are asked and the next morning I tell my wife I was unavoidably locked in a loft where I had been looking for bits of plaster. Males need to get out of themselves once in a while. Am I making myself clear?" I nodded.

"Besides, people interest me. They are ingenuous to a pleasant degree. I would miss New York were I to make a change. The chimes in the Metropolitan tower—they are mildly amusing; in a way, they get under my feathers. I have even composed words to go with them. Let it go—I won't bore you with them.

"I go frequently to Gramercy Park, which, as you know, is privately owned. Do you see the humor of it? Sparrows, flying over the fence and perching on the statue of Booth. Merely a crotchet. Have I answered your questions?"

"Yes," I said, "thanks."

"One other thing," the sparrow said. "You may quote me on this, if you like. The upper cables of the Brooklyn Bridge—they are incomparable! I go there for spiritual release. The town hangs like a crystal drip across the west. It gets up from the sea, erect, on an idea. Very likely a spurious idea—I don't know. *Au revoir.*"

"Wait a minute," I cried. "What about love—I forgot to ask."

"Why, I'm in love. Why not? Possibly a good thing at this fresh season; they are mulching the soil around the perennials in Union Square. Why shouldn't I shout? Come around in late September, you'll find me more myself."

And the sparrow was off, flying low toward infinity.

ASCENSION

3/17/28

THE MEMORY OF old Madison Square Garden still haunts the Square, but a very tangible and very beautiful building has arisen on the spot to dispel it. One of the stirring adventures of this windy Spring is to approach the still unfinished New York Life Insurance Building across the park, with the blue sky of morning for a backdrop. At first the tower, still a dark web of steel, seems predominant, with the supporting structure gleaming white, rising tier by tier, majestically. Then as you get nearer, the tower becomes lost to view behind the vast ramparts, which swim dizzily forward out of white clouds, and put you in your place.

A mighty climber ourself, we got permission to make the ascent the other morning, and after wandering through tomb-like depths peopled by a race of white and restless immortals who dwelt in a gloomy rain of plaster from above, we were inducted into an elevator made of a packing box, and hoisted twenty-three stories. The rest of the distance to the spidery tower was covered afoot, up dark stairs through interminable garrets that should have been full of old trunks and bats. To emerge, at last, on the hurricane deck, five hundred feet above reality, with no railing between us and the shimmering East River, with blocks of limestone pendulous about our head, with a whole new city of workmen trundling barrows of mortar, chipping stone, cutting tin, with blueprints aloft, with the canvas guards of the scaffolding bellying like sails in the breeze— this was a dream and a delight. "What time is it, buddy?" asked a red-headed bricklayer. "Ten of eleven," we replied, glancing down on the clock of the Metropolitan Tower.

Out of the strange confusion of dust and men was emerging, right under our feet, the modern pyramid—erect and without flaw and high. After five minutes, the sense of great altitude left us, and we discovered ourself peering inquisitively over the edge and poking around boldly on precipitous ledges. Workmen were nursing the great stone blocks into place, each dangling stone tended by a group of three men, while winch drivers sounded their rope signals and filled the air with bell-notes of progress. As the stones were eased down into seats of mortar and were levelled by eager-eyed constructionists, the whole thing grew, a perceptible upward thrust into the sky. It was magic of the most ethereal sort.

From the stone will rise a tall sloping tower of lead-coated copper, sparkling tourelles, and at the very peak (which an earthy little fellow in the engineer's office told us would be more than six hundred feet high) a bronze lantern.

It struck us, as we watched, that the workmen aloft there should find a mordant glee in rearing such a grand pile for the use of clerks who'll write policies for groundlings—to whom life, to be sweet, must be insured.

THE NEW YORK GARBAGEMAN

12/6/30

THERE IS NO ONE in all New York we envy more than the garbageman. Not even a fireman gets so much fun out of life. The jolly, jolly garbageman goes banging down the street without a thought for anyone. He clatters his cans as he listeth; he scatters ashes on the winds with never a thought that the wind-blown ash problem was settled in 1899 when the little old one-horse dump carts had covers put on them. He is shrewd in measuring his pace, and goes down the block bit by bit, innocently keeping just to windward of you. He drives like a ward boss through red lights and green, and backs his truck over the crossing with more privilege than a baby carriage on Fifth Avenue. He is as masterful as a pirate and chock-full of gusto. As we watch a garbage crew at work, we momentarily expect to see them burst into song and clink property beakers. Why shouldn't they? They have the town by the tail and they know it.

CROSSING THE STREET

7/16/32

POSSIBLY YOU HAVE NOTICED this about New Yorkers: instinctively, crossing a one-way street, they glance in the proper direction to detect approaching cars. They always know, without thinking, which way the traffic flows. They glance in the right direction as naturally as a deer sniffs upwind. Yet after that one glance in the direction from which the cars are coming, they always, just before stepping out into the street, also cast one small, quick, furtive look in the opposite direction— from which no cars could possibly come. That tiny glance (which we have noticed over and over again) is the last sacrifice on the altar of human fallibility; it is an indication that people can never quite trust the self-inflicted cosmos, and that they dimly suspect that some day, in the maze of well-regulated vehicles and strong, straight buildings, something will go completely crazy—something big and red and awful will come tearing through town going the wrong way on the one-ways, mowing down all the faithful and the meek. Even if it's only a fire engine.

VISITING MOTORISTS

12/2/33

FOR SIX DAYS of the week we find it no trouble at all to drive a car about town. New York's traffic, however furious, is predictable; and her taxis, even in moments of great verve, are accurate. For six days driving is a pleasure, but on Sundays all is changed: the town, we have discovered, fills up with visiting motorists who have come in from the Oranges and the Pelhams to see a movie. They make driving a hazard almost too great to take on. The minute a red light shows, they stop dead, imperiling everybody behind. The instant a taxi seems about to sideswipe them, they swerve desperately over and sideswipe somebody else, usually us. When they are confronted by a mass of pedestrians at the crossing, instead of charging boldly in and scattering them in the orthodox manner by sheer bluster (which is the only way), they creep timidly up blowing their horns, which lulls the pedestrians and ties up everything. They are easy to spot, these visiting motorists; and the only thing to do, we have found, is to nudge them frequently on the bumper, and chivy them about.

NEW YORK IN MARCH

3/2/35

THIS IS THE MOMENT in the year we are glad we're not on a tropical island, staring fatuously at a hibiscus flower or watching a lizard scale a white wall. The siren south is well enough, but New York, at the beginning of March, is a hoyden we would not care to miss—a drafty wench, her temperature up and down, full of bold promises and dust in the eye. There is a look in the clouds, a new power in the shafts of sun that tremble on the roofs of the "L" stations, a seductive whisper between snow flurries, an omen in the cold fire-escape shedding its skin. And when at five o'clock we emerge from the Library, where we are at work on a stark Northern proletarian novel called "So Rose the Red," we stand for a moment on the steps, looking through Forty-first Street to the chimneys in the east, and New York seems a wonderful brisk girl, whose arm we want to take on the way home.

Our deep affection for this galling and preposterous city is hard for some people to believe. Climatically New York amuses us; but an even stronger reason for the town's seeming habitable to us is that it is practically devoid of civic pride and wastes almost no time spreading its own gospel. At noon today the citizens of Mansfield, O., and Tacoma, Wash., will gather at luncheon clubs to bite the hard roll and taste the sweet *coupe municipale*. They will swat each other hopefully on the back and discover a mysterious significance in the latest realty report of freight-car loadings. Here, one doesn't hear the drumbeat at noontime. Our citizens have no notion of establishing, abetting, or recognizing any municipal puissance. When anybody brings up civic grandeur, New York bites its fingernails and gathers wool. Noons are given over to individual stomach disorders and private gain.

MOVING

10/5/35

GOADED BY restlessness and the delusion of greener pastures, we vacated an apartment where we had lived a long time. Four ape men, appearing in the steamy dawn, rolled up the mattresses, collapsed the beds, and with catlike tread removed all our effects, and our ineffects, to the inquisitive street and there wedged them into a red-devil horseless van. They stripped the place clean, to the eye. But as we sat on an empty fruit crate in the living-room, staring at the beloved walls with their unbleached rectangles where the pictures and mirrors had been, staring at the radiators whose first winter whisperings we will not hear this year, we knew that not even the stalwart movers could wrench loose something that was still there, invisible and ineradicable; we knew that people must inevitably leave something of themselves behind—something besides the mere residue of dust and bent paper clips and fallen coat hangers. We felt we should post a warning to the new tenants that there was something in the walls, musky and pervasive, as when a skunk vacates a nest under a summer cottage. There is sponginess about plaster, absorbing love. Not even a repaint job can quite rid a place of the people who once lived there.

There seems to be an uncommon amount of moving and shuffling about this October. Even old Mr. Eustace Tilley* has quit the pale-green diggings in West Forty-fifth Street where he lived in squalid terror for more than ten years, amid a rabble of importunate writers and artists. The old scamp was seen late one evening last week, his hat awry, his arms full of old wall mottoes, an andiron in his teeth and an unread poem tucked under his belt like a sword, sneaking through an arcade looking for new quarters. The load was too great: after a scant two blocks he gave up the search and took a year's lease near the top of a bleak redstone manse opposite the five-and-ten, where he can look out at the Harvard Club from the south, instead of from the north, and see directly into the mouths of patients in

---

*Fictional character representing *The New Yorker*; his portrait is reproduced each February on the cover of *The New Yorker* on the anniversary of its founding.

a dental school. Downstairs is the Life Extension Institute, and when they make too much noise down there, Tilley can be seen in one of his moods of magnificent irritation, drinking brandy neat and rapping on the floor with his cane.

Possessions breed like mice. A man forgets what a raft of irrelevant junk he has collected about him till he tries to move it. We found ourself one afternoon smothered at the bottom of a pile of ghastly miscellany: envelopes engraved with the wrong address, snapshots that had never been pasted up, a mahogany chip belonging to a broken chair, some high-school examination papers, a can of ski wax, several programs of the Millrose games,* a sneaker for the left foot, a build-it-yourself airplane that had never been built, some samples of curtain material, a catcher's mitt, and a red-and-silver ashtray made from the head of a piston. These objects suddenly seemed to be the possessor, ourself the possessed. An hour later we were wandering dully in the streets seeking lodging in a hotel and passed a little old fellow with all his worldly goods slung on his back in a burlap sack. In his face was written a strange peace.

THE LOOK OF A NATIVE

1/4/36

"HOW," writes a man from Atlanta (who perhaps has in mind coming to the Fair), "can a stranger in New York make himself *look* like a stranger, so that other strangers won't stop him on the street and ask a lot of questions about New York he can't answer?" That's an unusual question, and we doubt that it is an honest one. Actually, strangers ache to give the appearance of

*Indoor track competition at Madison Square Garden sponsored by the Millrose Athletic Association.

natives. The average New Yorker can spot a stranger in town easily. Strangers are extremely careful not to look up at tall buildings, for fear they will be spotted. They are unable to board a Fifth Avenue bus except after fearful experimentation. They overtip and are under the impression that the only places that sell theatre tickets are agencies.

Our own problem is to make ourself look like a New Yorker. Somehow, in spite of our fine clothes and worldly ways, nobody ever takes us for a native. Beggars, street photographers, men who have just located a nice fur piece, all spot us instantly as fair game. We are the perfect stranger. Probably it's because, although we have lived in New York all our life, the place never seems anything but slightly incredible, and we go along with our mouth open and our face unbuttoned.

WALKING TO WORK

2/13/37

FROM OUR HOME in the cinder belt to this Forty-third Street pent-up house where we work is a distance of some nine blocks—in a southwesterly direction. It has sometimes occurred to us that we take an unconscionably long time walking it, the time ranging from fifteen minutes to two hours and a half. Three-quarters of an hour is about par. This morning, arriving at work at eleven-thirty, after being on the road for more than an hour, we felt that perhaps we should attempt to reconstruct the journey to see what the hell went on when we were supposed to be covering ground. There were dim memories of many uninspired shop windows, including an imaginary decision involving a pair of madras pajamas, as between the gray with the narrow stripes and the deep blue. There was a pleasant ten minutes standing quietly with others of our ilk, watching a taxi that had hooked onto a limousine, watching the lady in the limousine pretending she had not been hooked onto by the middle classes.

There was the slow, steady perusal of a small bag of humus in front of a flower shop (ten cents) and the weighing of the question whether to buy it now—which would mean lugging it both to and from work—or to buy it on the way home, with the strong chance that we'd forget to. There was the pause in front of the art shop's nude-of-the-day, in company with the gray little group of men (art lovers all), each of us trying to look as though we were interested in gum erasers and T squares. There was the slowing of pace in front of Charles & Ernest's, to see who was getting his hair cut today. There was the pastry shop, with its fascinating handling of yet undigested material. There was Abercrombie's, effeteness blended with woodcraft; the side trip into the bookshop to examine new titles; the side trip to Radio City to see how the ice looked; the pause while two cats stared each other down in a parking lot. (And, incidentally, why will men stop and watch cats carrying on; women never? Is it because a tom is an unmistakable rake?)

Our reconstructed journey was not encouraging. The wonder is we arrived at all.

THE LURE OF NEW YORK

7/3/37

THE INQUIRING PHOTOGRAPHER of the *Daily News* stopped six people the other day and asked them why they loved New York. He got six different answers. One lady said she loved New York because it was vibrant. One man said he loved it because business was good here. These replies made us think of the fine, clear answer which a friend of ours, a Greek shoe-black, once gave to the same question. This gentleman had got sick of New York, had wearied of his little shoe-and-hat parlor with its smell of polish and gasoline, and had gone back to his native island of Keos, where, he told us, he would just swim and fish and lie in the grass while beautiful girls fed him fruit. He was back in town in about four months. We asked him what there was about this city, what mysterious property, that had lured him back from the heaven that was Keos. He thought for a minute. Then he said, "In New York you can buy things so late at night."

NEW YORK SOIL

9/30/50

AS WE GO TO PRESS we discover that the Friends of the Land are about to hold their harvest-home supper right here in town, in the Statler, across from the depot. Louis Bromfield, the dirt farmer, and Dr. Hugh Bennett, chief of the Soil Conservation Service, are scheduled to speak. We don't know what the soil is like down there near the Statler but it is probably a heavy clay with a lot of Consolidated Edison roots that haven't rotted up yet, and it undoubtedly needs top dressing to bring it back. This is a good month to top-dress, and there is no better man on a manure spreader than Bromfield.

If the Friends of the Land weren't so numerous, we would invite them to our apartment and take them to our bedroom, so they could look out the window by our desk and study a most inspiring example of Nature's soil-building. Just outside the window there is a stone coping that forms the top of a high wall. Three years ago an ailanthus seed came to rest on this bare ledge twenty feet above the ground. Encouraged by light rains and heavy sootfall, it germinated. Its root immediately struck solid rock, turned quickly, and found two dead vine leaves, a cigarette butt, and a paper clip. Here were perfect conditions for ailanthus growth. The little tree sprang toward heaven. Through a long, dry summer, watered by occasional fogs from the East River, nourished by mop dust and the slow drift of falling vine leaves, the sapling took hold. Today it stands a stalwart forest giant, as big around as our thumb, lively as a grig, covering its roots a living soil rich in those minerals and organic substances that only the fairest city in the world can scrape together to take care of its own.

NEW YORK'S COCKTAIL

1/30/54

THIS IS A DAY of fog and smoke in equal parts—a city cocktail familiar to all, the pure ingredient contributed by nature, the poisonous one contributed by Man, the mixture served slightly chilled, with a twist of irony. On our way to the office we heard complaints on every hand: the barber, the bus driver, the store-keeper, the elevator operator, all of them clearing their throats nervously, each indignant that pure air was denied him. One of them said, "Nobody does anything. Maybe you write a letter to the paper and it gets printed—so what happens? Nothing." The city has a debased feeling on its smog days, ill temper and foul air combining to form an unwholesomeness. Buildings fade out in their upper reaches, escarpments grow soft in the yellow haze. Chimneys discharge sable smoke in luscious folds, as when the rich intestines of an animal are exposed by the slaughterer's knife, and the sulphurous smoke, curling upward, quickly feels the control of the ceiling, turns, and drifts down instead, filling streets, alleys, areaways, parks, sifting through windows and doors, entering the rooms and the offices, even invading the oxygen tents where patients struggle for breath. Being in the city on such a day is like waiting, condemned, in a lethal chamber for the release that has not yet come. Certainly no other animal fouls its nest so cheerfully and persis-tently as Man, or acts so surprised and sore about it afterward. Everywhere common sense and general welfare await the in-dulgence of the special business and the particular chimney.

COPING WITH SOOTFALL

9/11/54

A PLAN TO BUILD an outdoor dining terrace at the headquarters of the United Nations, in Turtle Bay, has been abandoned because of "atmospheric conditions"—which is a diplomatic term for sootfall. We happen to be a student of atmospheric conditions in Turtle Bay, having dwelt there happily for many years, and we can testify that sootfall does not preclude terrace life if you have any guts. Our own terrace—a small, decadent structure a few blocks from the U. N.—is a howling success as far as we are concerned, and we are in a good position to give the U. N. a few helpful hints on terrace living under heavy sootfall. First of all, you have to get an awning. The awning is not to ward off soot but merely to give the terrace dweller a cozy feeling. It soon catches fire from cigarettes tossed out of upper windows, but the fire is a clubby affair and you get to know your neighbors (a valuable experience for the United Nations, if you ask us). Next, you've got to have a glass-top table and some iron chairs with little thin detachable cushions that fade. Every time you come indoors from the terrace, even if only for a moment, you pick up your cushion and heave it ahead of you through the open door into the living room. If you leave a drink standing on the table to go inside and answer the phone, you simply drape your handkerchief over the glass, and when you come back you dump the soot out of the handkerchief and resume drinking. If the drinks are properly mixed, the soot can lie roundabout, deep and crisp and even, and nobody will mind. Soot is the topsoil of New York, giving plants a foothold, or soothold, on ramparts far above street level. We have a five-year-old ailanthus, a lovely tree, rooted in soot, and we are shocked and discouraged at the capitulation of the United Nations in the face of this mild threat—an organization created to bring peace to the world yet scared to death that some tiny foreign particle is going to fall into its drink.

THE RAMBLE

7/30/55

JUST SOUTH OF the Seventy-ninth Street transverse in the Park, and lying between the East Drive and the West Drive, there is a tract of wild land called the Ramble. Like most urban jungles, it has a somewhat shabby appearance. It is thickly wooded and rocky, and in the middle of it there is a miniature swamp. Paths twist and turn back upon themselves and peter out in dirt trails leading down to the shores of the Seventy-second Street Lake. Except for one peculiarity, the Ramble is no different from dozens of fairly green mansions inside the city limits. What distinguishes it is the fact that, in the magical moments of migration, birds descend into the place in great numbers and in almost unbelievable variety. They ignore other attractive areas in the Park and drop straight into the Ramble. The reason is simple. The place offers good cover and it has water, the two requisites for the peace of mind of small songsters. Because of its phenomenal popularity among transient birds, the Ramble is known to ornithologists and nature students all over the world. They, too, dive straight into it when they come to New York.

On a hot, airless afternoon recently, we went up to the Park to take what may be our last look at the Ramble. The place has been marked for "improvement" by the Commissioner of Parks,* who plans to unscramble the Ramble, comb its hair, and build a recreation center there for old people—shuffleboard, croquet, television, lawns, umbrella tables, horse-shoe pitching, the works. This strikes us as an unnecessary blunder. Almost any place in Central Park would lend itself to shuffleboard, but the Ramble has lent itself to more than two hundred species of travelling birds. It is truly a fabulous little coppice. On a still summer's day, it is nothing to write home about; we found it populated by grackles, house sparrows, rats, gray squirrels, lovers, and one gnarled old editorial writer creeping sadly about. But on a morning in May the Ramble is alive with bright song and shy singers. (Soon it

*Robert Moses, New York City's Commissioner of Parks.

will ring with early TV commercials and the click of quoits.)

The conversion of the Ramble from a wild place to a civilized place, from an amazingly successful bird cover in the heart of the city to a gaming court, raises a fundamental question in Park administration. City parks are queer places at best; they must provide a green escape from stone and steel, and they must also provide amusement for the escapees—everything from zoos to swings, from ball fields to band shells. The original design of Central Park emphasized nature. The temptation has been to encroach more and more on the jungle. And the temptation grows stronger as more and more citizens die and leave money for memorial structures. It seems to us that if it's not too late, Mr. Moses should reconsider the matter of the Ramble and find another site for oldsters and their fun-making.

Robert Cushman Murphy, birdman emeritus of the American Museum of Natural History, wrote a letter to the *Times* not long ago on this subject. Mr. Murphy made the following statement: "There is probably no equal area of open countryside that can match the urban-bounded Ramble with respect to the concentration of birds that funnels down from the sky just before daybreaks of spring." Think of it! This minuscule Manhattan wildwood taking first place in the daybreaks of spring! It is no trick to outfit a public park for our winter mornings, our fall afternoons, our summer evenings. But the daybreaks of spring—what will substitute for the Ramble when that happy circumstance is tossed away?

TUMBLEWEED

2/23/57

IN A HALF-DESERTED STREET, on a day of high wind, a discarded Christmas tree came bearing down on us, rolling rapidly. "Tumbleweed!" we muttered, dodging to one side, and were suddenly transported to the Western plains and experienced again, after so many years, the excitement of our first meeting with the weed. New York seems able to reproduce almost any natural phenomenon if it's in the mood.

NEW YORK

6/11/55

THE TWO MOMENTS when New York seems most desirable, when the splendor falls all round about and the city looks like a girl with leaves in her hair, are just as you are leaving and must say goodbye, and just as you return and can say hello. We had one such moment of infatuation not long ago on a warm, airless evening in town, before taking leave of these shores to try another city and another country for a while. There seemed to be a green tree overhanging our head as we sat in exhaustion. All day the fans had sung in offices, the air-conditioners had blown their clammy breath into the rooms, and the brutal sounds of demolition had stung the ear—from buildings that were being knocked down by the destroyers who have no sense of the past. Above our tree, dimly visible in squares of light, the city rose in air. From an open window above us, a whiff of perfume or bath powder drifted down startlingly in the heavy night, somebody having taken a tub to escape the heat. On the tips of some of the branches, a few semiprecious stars settled themselves to rest. There was nothing about the occasion that distinguished it from many another city evening, nothing in particular that we can point to to corroborate our emotion. Yet we somehow tasted New York on our tongue in a great, overpowering draught, and felt that to sail away from so intoxicating a place would be unbearable, even for a brief spell.

14

Whims

CERTAINTIES

1/9/37

SEATED BETWEEN TWO INTELLECTUAL giants after dinner, we were borne lightly along on conversation's wave, from country to country, dipping into problems of empire, the rise and fall of dynasties, the loves and hates of kings, the warrings in Spain, the trends in Russia, strikes, revolutions, diplomacies, the dissolution of peoples; and without a pause heard everything under the sun made plain. We have the deepest envy for anyone who can feel at home with great matters, and who, armed cap-a-pie with information, can see into the motives of rulers and the hearts of subjects, and can answer Yes to this, No to that. Our envy was so strong that when we returned home at midnight and our wife asked us whether, in our opinion, our dog had worms, we answered with a bold Yes, in a moment of vainglory pretending that here was a thing on which we spoke knowingly—though such was far from the case, as we both secretly knew.

SEPARATIONS

6/13/31

IN THE SHORT SPACE of half a block, coming home from lunch, one encounters enough human dismay to keep one from getting any work done all the rest of the afternoon. In a building that had two entrances we happened to see, in one entrance, a girl waiting with apparent impatience and disappointment for somebody we suspected was a man, and in the other entrance a man waiting with just as great disappointment for somebody we didn't doubt was a girl. Whether to go up to one of them and whisper: "Go to the other entrance"—that was a problem for a noonday pedestrian who worries, as we do, about life's haphazards. Further along the block, another incident—this time we happened to encounter a kiss. Not a snippy, worn-out kiss, but an important emotional kiss of longing or promise. It was meant to be a kiss in parting, but the trouble was that in attempting to part, the two got held up by crosstown traffic, and had to stand right where they were in a silly fashion, waiting for the cars to pass before they could go their separate and significant ways. This spoiled the kiss and the occasion.

SALUTATIONS

9/19/31

STRANGE AS IT MAY SEEM, we continue to receive letters from people interested in the problem—broached by us last June—of the correct salutation to use in a letter to a girls' school. (Whether to begin "Dear Ladies," or "My Dears," or what.) First there is a communication from Thomas O. Mabbott, Ph.D., assistant professor at Hunter College, who says that the head of his department writes "Dear Colleagues." Appeals for contributions, he says, are likely to employ the feminine pronoun in the body of the text. An etiquette writer in the *World-Telegram,* propounding the same problem, by a funny coincidence, advises the use of the French "Mesdames," followed, the writer goes on, "by the customary dash." A man in Baltimore writes that the Governor of the Virgin Islands once wrote a letter to Goucher College beginning: "To the director of one group of virgins from another," which we neither believe nor think funny. A doctor's secretary writes that she was once faced with a similar problem answering a letter from a divine who had signed himself "Your brother in Christ." She saw no way out except to begin: "Dear Buddy." Our liveliest communication, however, was from a School and Camp Specialist—a lady who not only claimed that she could tell, by glancing at her files, the sex of every school principal, matron, dean, or trustee in the country, but that furthermore her office was situated right across the street from ours and that if ever we were really stuck for a salutation, we might write the name of the school on a large piece of cardboard, hold it at the window, and she would gladly flash back the sex of the principal. There, we felt, was help.

LINDBERGH'S GLORY

5/28/27

THE LONELY MR. LINDBERGH made the hop without a cup of coffee. This fact alone startled fifty million Americans who have never been able to get through a working day without one. Furthermore, the flyer came down in France without saying that he did it for the kiddies—un-American and unusual. We loved him immediately.

We noted that the *Spirit of St. Louis* had not left the ground ten minutes before it was joined by the Spirit of Me Too. A certain oil was lubricating the engine, a certain brand of tires was the cause of the safe take-off. When the flyer landed in Paris every newspaper was "first to have a correspondent at the plane." This was a heartening manifestation of that kinship that is among man's greatest exaltations. It was beautifully and tenderly expressed by the cable Ambassador Herrick sent the boy's patient mother: "Your incomparable son has done me the honor to be my guest." We liked that; and for twenty-four hours the world seemed pretty human. At the end of that time we were made uneasy by the volume of vaudeville contracts, testimonial writing and other offers, made by the alchemists who transmute glory into gold. We settled down to the hope that the youthful hero will capitalize himself for only as much money as he reasonably needs.

DISILLUSION

2/16/29

AS WE GROW OLDER, we find ourself groping toward things that give us a sense of security. Grimly we hang to anything firm, immutable. For that reason we've always set great store by clocks in telegraph offices—other clocks could say what they pleased; to us a clock in a telegraph office was in tune with the planets, was Time Itself. So when we happened to pass a Postal Telegraph office the other morning and saw a great palpable lie written across the face of its clock, life seemed to slip away treacherously from under our feet, and the Naval Observatory (to us a vast marble hall set in concrete on a mountain) slowly crumbled before our eyes, a wet and dripping ruin in a bog of quicksand.

HIPPODROME

2/9/29

THERE IS SOMETHING ineffably melancholy about the senescence of the Hippodrome—that once gorgeous place. Lately it has catered to the Sixth Avenue trade with such gray trifles as movies, sword swallowers, and pieces of the Wright Whirlwind motors on display in the lobby. Although we know by reading the papers that Sarah Bernhardt, Billy Sunday, and Captain George Fried have trod the Hippodrome's boards, we happen to belong to the generation to whom the Hippodrome means only one thing—the place where, in the long ago, marvellously beautiful maidens used to walk down a flight of stairs into the water, remain for several minutes, and later appear dripping and nymphlike from the unthinkable depths. Incidentally, it is the mansion where we lost, forever, our childlike faith in our father's all-embracing knowledge; for when we asked him point-blank what happened to the ladies while they were under the water, his answer was so vague, so evasive, so palpably out of accord with even the simplest laws of physics, that even our child mind sensed its imbecility, and we went our way thereafter alone in the world, seeking for truth.

OLD COAT

10/24/31

"IT IS NOT EVERY MAN," our tailor writes, "that can afford to wear a shabby coat." He hit home; for a shabby coat is our one extravagance, the one luxury we have been able to affect. Four winters, now, we have crept about the streets in the cold unkempt security of a battered Burberry—a thin, inadequate garment, pneumonia written in every seam, a disreputable coat, the despair of friends, the byword of enemies, a coat grown so gossamerlike in texture that merely to catch sight of it hanging in the closet is to feel the chill in one's marrows. What its peculiar charm is we don't quite know—whether it is a sop to inelegance, a faint bid for a lost virility, or the simple gesture of the compleat snob. Whatever its hold on us, it has gradually acquired the authentic gentility of an old lady's limousine, but without any of the limousine's protection against draughts. All we know is that every icy blast that grips our blue abdomen, every breeze that climbs the shin, feeds the dying fires of our once great spirit; and that as we shrink deeper into the shabbiness of this appalling garment, we find a certain contentment that no tailor could possibly afford us, for all his engraved announcements.

COLONIZATION

5/23/36

AMONG THE UNACCEPTED INVITATIONS that have been kicking around our desk for a couple of weeks is one asking us if we would like to become a member of an island colony—a place "where eugenic considerations would always be central." The letter seems to be from a Mr. Elmer Pendell, of DuBois, Pa., who points out that the typical community in America has now become atrophied and it is high time for us to colonize another land. He is not without his reasonable doubts as to the success of any such venture, for he candidly poses certain questions. "Would we," he asks us, "need to make arrangements to supply tobacco, coffee, tea, wine, beer, salt, pepper, other spices—or could these or some of them be left out?" It is the kind of challenge that keeps us pacing around our room when we should be at our work—pacing, pacing, wondering whether we could be eugenic without mace, whether we could pioneer sans paprika.

FRONTIER

A NOTE HAS ARRIVED from the Department of the Interior regarding the Great Smokies, last frontier of the East. Secretary Ickes,* it appears, has decided that the characteristics and habits of the mountain folk must be preserved, along with other natural features of the region—birds, trees, animals. A student of linguistics is at work collecting songs and ballads, and there is a definite movement afoot to encourage the Great Smoky people to continue speaking and acting in a distinctly Early American manner.

Our government, with its youthful hopes and fears, is sometimes hard to follow. Mr. Roosevelt has dwelt at length on the plight of the underprivileged third—ill-housed, ill-clad, ill-nourished. But this note from Ickes describes a toothless old grandmother who, though she sleeps on a cornhusk bed and wears no shoes, is apparently the Ideal Woman of the Interior Department. They want to preserve her just as she is—her speech, her homespun garments, her bare feet, her primitive customs, even her rebellious nature (she doesn't like the North). Well, who's right? If business is to revive, this old lady has got to buy our American products; she's got to spruce up her person and her home. She's got to have an electric orange-squeezer and a suitable tray for serving canapés. She's got to quit grinding her own meal and buy herself a bag of Gold Medal. She's got to trade the ox for a Pontiac, and she certainly must quit talking like a hick and get herself a radio, so that she can hear the pure accents of the American merchandiser. Yet if she does, the Great Smokies will be spoiled for Ickes and presumably for the rest of us. What quaint mountains will we drive to, in our restless sedans? What hillbilly program will we tune in on, with our insatiable radios? Truly, a nation in search of a frontier is in the devil of a fine fix.

---

*Harold L. Ickes, Secretary of the Interior 1933–46 and director of the Public Works Administration 1933–39.

BARRYMORE'S IDEAL

8/26/39

WE WERE GLAD TO LEARN in the *Mirror* that John Barrymore has never been in love in his life but is still in search of the Ideal Woman. This incurable romantic streak in Mr. Barrymore, which enables him to be both discourteous to the four women of his ex-choice and idealistic toward the yet unattained she, is a challenge to all males. Furthermore, Mr. Barrymore gave the reporter who interviewed him a description of his ideal, a description which enriches and enlarges the field of American love. He said her aura of glamour would trump the noonday sun, her oomph would be a symphony of tuba horns. With this definition from a member of the Royal Family, Love emerges from old moon-haunted glades and comes out into the broiling sun, where it belongs, among mad dogs and Englishmen. Hark, Chloë, is that the sound of distant tubas?

BOAT SHOWS

1/19/52

THE HEAVIEST CONCENTRATION of New York's dream life is almost certainly to be found under the roof at the annual Boat Show. Here is where more men can gaze at what they are never going to possess than in any other gathering. A man who is born boat-happy dies boat-happy, and the intervening years are a voyage that may never take him afloat but that keeps him alive. Much of the time, he is in exquisite torture from unfulfilled desire, and spends his hours reading books about the sea. The boating world contains, of course, tiny coracles that are cheap enough to be within the means of practically anybody. But it also contains, as many a man knows, the dream ship that is always just out of sight over the horizon. The second-hand market is not much help. A good boat, strongly built and well maintained, doesn't depreciate greatly in value, as a car does, and a man may wait thirty years to realize his dream, only to find that by the time he is wealthy enough to buy the boat, he has become too emaciated to hoist sail and get the anchor. A man feels about a boat entirely differently from the way he feels about a car: he falls in love with it, often from afar, and the affair is a secret one—comparable to that of a young girl who sleeps with an actor's photograph under her pillow. Many an otherwise normal man falls in love with a boat at the age of fourteen, guards his secret well, and dies with it; and the boat is just as beautiful, her profile as lovely, her sheer line as tantalizing, at the time of his death as at the beginning of the affair. When you encounter this poor fellow in Grand Central Palace, poking around among the booths and twiddling with the sheaves of blocks, you would never suspect him of being the Great Lover that he is. He looks just like the next man—which isn't surprising, for the next man is suffering too.

LEISURE CLASS

8/8/53

WE RAN ACROSS the phrase "leisure class" the other day and it stopped us cold, so quaint did it sound, so fragrant with the spice of yesteryear. You used to read a good deal about the leisure class, but something seems to have happened to it. One thing that may have happened to it is that too many people joined it and the point went out of it. In the big cities, everybody quits work now on Friday, climbs into a car, and beats it. That much is sure. Where these elusive people go we aren't quite sure, but they do go away, and presumably on the wings of leisure. A switchboard operator disappears from the switchboard on a Friday, and the next time you see her a lot of water has gone over the dam and she is unrecognizable because of leisure and exposure to the sun, which serves all classes equally. If your refrigerator quits making ice cubes on a Saturday afternoon (as ours did recently) or if you lose a gall bladder on Times Square after the Saturday-evening show, you might just as well walk over to the river, tie a rock to your foot, and jump in. Your repairman and your doctor are in the Catskills, probably fishing from the same boat. The few glimpses we have had lately of highways, beaches, and mountain-house porches have not been reassuring; these are the classic habitats of the leisure class, but the scenes have been confused and incredibly scrambled, like an infield during a bunt. Leisure used to have a direct relationship to wealth, but even that seems to have changed. A lot of people who are independently wealthy cannot properly claim to belong to the leisure class anymore: they are too nerved up to be leisurely and too heavily taxed to be completely relieved of the vulgar burden of finding a livelihood. They, too, swarm out of town on Friday, along with their switchboard operator, and they show up again a few days later, burned and exhausted, ready for another short, feverish period of steady gain, at desk, at dictaphone, at wit's end.

15

Endings and Farewells

IMMORTALITY

3/28/36

THE PUBLISHERS of a forthcoming volume of poetry have advised us that by subscribing to it we can have our name "incorporated into the front matter of the book" along with the names of the other subscribers. This, of course, would immortalize us as a person who once read a book—or at any rate as a person who once *intended* to read a book. It is not the sort of immortality we crave, our feeling being that deathlessness should be arrived at in a more haphazard fashion. Loving fame as much as any man, we shall carve our initials in the shell of a tortoise and turn him loose in a peat bog.

THE LIFE TRIUMPHANT

7/17/43

THERE IS A MAN in Indianapolis named William H. Fine, who writes me letters calling me a quitter. I have suffered under the sting of his lash for two or three years without saying anything in my own defense, but the time has come to reply. I am not a quitter and I feel that such a charge could be brought against me only by a person who is not in possession of the facts. Briefly, the facts are these:

I came to Fine's attention in the late nineteen-thirties, when I won a contest sponsored by a beer concern. I had to supply the last line of a poem and I did it satisfactorily. The prize was ten dollars. My success aroused Fine's interest, although he was clear out in Indianapolis, and he wrote congratulating me on my work and introducing himself as "America's Foremost Contest Counselor." Letter followed letter, and soon he had changed his tune and was upbraiding me for lying back on my oars after my early show of promise. Just this morning I heard from him again. His letter began, "A quitter never won anything but regrets" and then went on to describe the two distinct types of service Fine offers to contestants to enable them to win prize money. One type is for persons who enter contests regularly, persons for whom Fine has a real affection. The other type is for the flash-in-the-pan sort, the sort Fine thinks I am, the sort who wins one contest and then rests on his laurels. Fine prefers a plodder with guts and perseverance to a merely talented man who lacks staying quality.

The whole thing would be laughable if it were any charge but "quitting." Fine assumes, somewhat presumptuously, that he knows all about me. He has sized me up as a one-timer, a one-prize Johnny. The plain fact is, I am a prize-winning fool, victor of a score of contests. Fine just happened to run across me in the beer job, but he was thirty years late. I began winning prizes in 1909, have been at it steadily ever since, and expect to win many more in years to come. At the moment I am vacillating between the Alexander Smith & Sons Carpet Co.'s thousand-dollar award for the best letter on "How We Hope to Fix Up Our Home After the War" and the Harper ten-thousand-dollar prize for the best novel by a writer who had not been published prior to January 1, 1924. I shall enter one or the other. But that's in the future, of course, and has an element of uncertainty about it, whereas the past, my past, is something else again. My past is a kaleidoscope in which triumph follows triumph in intricate patterns of prodigious light. My past is an open book, which Fine obviously has not taken the trouble to read.

The first award I ever received for meritorious work was from the *Woman's Home Companion*. The year, as I say, was 1909, or "Oughty Nine" as it was then known. The prize was a copy of "Rab and His Friends," by John Brown, M.D. I can't seem to recall what I had to do to win it, but I think likely it was a literary contest. I was something of a writer in those days, as well as a dabbler in the other arts. I still have the postcard which brought me the tidings of that first victory. It is signed "Aunt Janet." "Assuring you of my constant interest in your work and hoping to see more of it from time to time, Very affectionately, Aunt Janet."

Well, what about that, Fine?

What about the silver badge I copped from the St. Nicholas League?* What about the gold badge? Let me see your badge, Fine! I have a feeling you never even won honorable mention in the puzzles division. Who are you, anyway, to be calling me a quitter?

My next smashing success in the contest world came in my high-school days. New York State (or it might have been Cornell University, I can't seem to remember which) was holding out a pretty plum to the winners of a special examination which had been trumped up out of the entire field of human knowledge. The prize was six hundred dollars' worth of tuition, or fun, at Ithaca. There were four of these prizes to be distributed, one to each assembly district. I took the exam and finished in fifth place, which would have left me out in the cold but for a most unusual and suspicious occurrence. It seems, Fine, that somebody had just divided one of the assembly districts in two, making five districts. A quick stroke of the pen on a wall map somewhere, and I drew the six hundred dollars. That's the kind of contestant I am, buddies with Lady Luck, my mouth bulging with silver spoons. I have never known who was responsible for cutting the district in two but have always assumed it was one of my relatives. We were a close bunch and pulled together. Still, it was none of my business and I never pried into it.

The prize money took me to college, where I would have gone anyway, as I was a well-heeled little customer who had gone after the scholarship from pure greed. At Cornell I promptly set to work entering other contests. I went out for track, and I am sorry to say, Fine, that in this particular field your accusation is justified: I quit track. I quit all right, but it wasn't because I couldn't run fast, it was on account of a pair of track shoes I had bought from a merchant named Dick Couch. They didn't fit, that's the long and short of it. Whenever

*The silver badge was for "A Winter Walk," published in *St. Nicholas*, June 1911: 757; the gold badge was for "A True Dog Story," *St. Nicholas*, Sept. 1914: 1045.

I wore them I was in torture, and I kept trying to persuade Couch to change them for another pair but he never would, so I spent all my time racing between Couch's store and my room in North Baker Hall and never had time to participate in any of the formal athletic contests. Of course, it is not for me to say that I would have won any of those races. Nevertheless, I was a swift thing on two legs and as light as a feather.

What about the way I came through with the winning sonnet in the Bowling Green contest in the old New York *Evening Post*? Surely you didn't miss that tourney, Fine? The track experience had been a hard blow but it didn't break my spirit and I did *not* quit. I was right in there pitching when Christopher Morley announced a sonnet contest. The prize was a book—one of his own, as a matter of fact. If you have never read that sonnet, Fine, get it and read it.* It will take your breath away. Meritorious as all hell. Fourteen big lines, every one of them a money-winner. Quitter, eh? Quitter my eye. Have you ever written a sonnet when your feet were killing you? A man who can go four years with a pair of track shoes that bind him across the toe and still turn out a workmanlike poem is no quitter. Not in my dull lexicon.

What about the first horse I ever bet on? That was in Lexington, Kentucky, where I had gone to seek my fortune in an atmosphere favorable to the competitive spirit. (I had held three or four jobs around New York that winter, but they were prosy things at best and I felt I was losing my fine edge so I got out.) My first horse was a female named Auntie May. She was an odd-looking animal and an eleven-to-one shot, but there was this to be said for her—she came in first. Perhaps you are the type of man, Fine, who doesn't recognize betting as a contest. You would if you had to run around the track twice, the way the horses did. Kentucky was lovely that spring. I got twenty-two dollars from the contest and would have let it go at that if I had not chanced to fall in with some insatiable people who were on their way to Louisville to enter other contests. Sport of kings, Fine. I went along with them. It seems I got hooked in Louisville. The Derby was a little too big for me, I guess. Easy come, easy go. But I didn't quit. I was temporarily without money but I still had a sonnet or two up my sleeve. After the

*"Bantam and I," *New York Evening Post* 17 Nov. 1923: 10.

226

race I returned to my hotel (I didn't say I was registered there, I said I returned to my hotel) and wrote a fourteen-line tribute to Morvich, the winning horse, and later that evening sold it to a surprised but accommodating city editor. If you will look in the Louisville *Herald* for Sunday, May 14, 1922, you will find my sonnet and will see how a young, inexperienced man can lose a horse race but still win enough money to get out of town. You needn't thumb all through the paper, Fine, it's right on the front page, in a two-column box.

Kentucky was indeed lovely that spring. Exhausted from my successes and my trials, I spent quite a while just wandering around the state and will always remember one little valley where the whippoorwills—but don't let me digress.

My next contest was in Minneapolis. True to form I blew into town just as a limerick contest was in full swing. I came through magnificently. The Minneapolis *Journal* was offering twenty-five dollars for a last line for a limerick, and I had that knack. A man has to live. The *Journal* was in search of a suitable conclusion for the following limerick:

> A young man who liked to rock boats
> In order to get people's goats
> Gave just one more rock
> Then suffered a shock

To thousands of residents of Minneapolis, this was a poser, but it was just my oyster. I sent in the surefire line "A bubble the spot now denotes." It rhymed, it was the right metre, and it was catchy. It had the mark on it of an experienced prize-winner. Apparently there was no question among the judges, once they came upon it. From among the thousands of other entries, it stood out as though etched in flame. The money was very welcome, when I received it, and as a matter of fact I could have used fifty rather than twenty-five, because I managed to dislocate my elbow about that time (no contest, just straight sailing) and was in the clutches of a medical man. I often think of those other Minneapolitans who got only honorable mention from all the effort they put into that contest—Stephen H. Brown, O. A. Glasow, Minnie R. Long, V. M. Arbogast, M. D. Rudolph. Talented people, all of them, but lacking that curious spark that touches off a genuine money-winner.

*

After my Minneapolis triumph there was a lapse of several years, a dull period, Fine, when I lay fallow and roused myself only long enough to produce a few listless pentameters in praise of coffee for some sort of promotion scheme cooked up by the caffeine interests. But once a contestant always a contestant. In 1929 I was again active in prize circles. I won the gold watch offered by Franklin P. Adams for the best "Conning Tower" poem of the year.* What if the watch doesn't keep time any more, I won it, didn't I? Who wants to know what time it is? It's no trick, in this world, to find out what time it is—you can glance into any barbershop—the trick is to win something. Then the beer concern came along and I ran away with that. The end is not in sight. About a year ago I spent a good deal of time working on the Ten Crown Activated Charcoal Gum gold-watch award for the best line to go with "Ten Crown Gum Helps Keep Teeth White" but got distracted by the Harper-125th-anniversary-twelve-thousand-dollar prize for the best piece of non-fiction. I hung fire so long I missed the bus in both contests. Chewing gum got scarce and the Ten Crown people either went off the air entirely or else my battery set got so run down I couldn't hear it any more, and the Harper offer expired.

This year, as I say, I am hesitating between the Alex Smith Dream Home contest and the Harper fiction thing. As I write this, I have only sixteen days to go on the Harper novel, but I have thought of a last line and I figure that if a man has a good last line he can build up the preliminary stuff in short order. I am also in line for an award from "Information Please"—they still have a question of mine. I asked them if they could tell the difference between a sow, a shoat, a boar, a pig, a hog, a gilt, and a barrow. So far they have not used the question and I can only assume that it is a little too hard for them. They're always shying away from things they don't know and getting back to Gilbert and Sullivan.

Well, I have spread my record before you, Fine. I'm not making any exorbitant claims for myself. In fact, I'm just an ordinary fellow in many ways, but I want to make it plain that

*"The Twentieth Century Gets Through," *New York World* 4 Dec. 1929: 13.

this is not the record of a quitter and I shall expect you to stop
using that word about me. When I decide to quit in the great
contest of life, I'll drop you a card. Maybe I'll sign it Aunt Janet.
Meantime, I'll thank you to mind your manners.

DOOMSDAY

11/17/45

THE WORLD, says Wells,* is at the end of its tether. "The end
of everything we call life is close at hand," he writes in his last
literary statement, distributed by International News Service.
We note, however, that Mr. Wells went to the trouble of taking
out a world copyright on his world's-end article. A prophet who
was firmly convinced that the jig was up wouldn't feel any need
of protecting his rights. We charge Mr. Wells with trying to
play doom both ways.

Wells has been a good prophet, as prophets go, and his crys-
tal-gazing is not to be sniffed at. And even lesser prophets,
these days, can feel that "frightful queerness" that he says has
come into life. At the risk, however, of seeming to suggest the
continuance of life on earth, we must admit that we found the
Wells article unconvincing in places. It is not clear yet, at any
rate, whether the world is at the end of its tether or whether
Wells is merely at the end of his. His description is not so much
of the end of life in the world as of the end of his ability to figure
life out. The two are not necessarily identical.

Wells is seventy-nine, and it is possible, of course, that he
confuses his own terminal sensations with universal twilight,
and that his doom is merely a case of mistaken identity. Most
writers find the world and themselves practically interchange-

*H. G. Wells, *Mind at the End of Its Tether* (London: Heinemann, 1945).

able, and in a sense the world dies every time a writer dies, because, if he is any good, he has been wet nurse to humanity during his entire existence and has held earth close around him, like the little obstetrical toad that goes about with a cluster of eggs attached to his legs. We hope Mr. Wells is wrong for once and that man is not the suicide he looks at the moment. Man is unpredictable, despite Mr. Wells' good record. On Monday, man may be hysterical with doom, and on Tuesday you will find him opening the Doomsday Bar & Grill and settling down for another thousand years of terrifying queerness.

H. W. ROSS

12/15/51

ROSS* DIED IN BOSTON, unexpectedly, on the night of December 6th, and we are writing this in New York (unexpectedly) on the morning of December 7th. This is known, in these offices that Ross was so fond of, as a jam. Ross always knew when we were in a jam, and usually got on the phone to offer advice and comfort and support. When our phone rang just now, and in that split second before the mind focusses, we thought, "Good! Here it comes!" But this old connection is broken beyond fixing. The phone has lost its power to explode at the right moment and in the right way.

Actually, things are not going as badly as they might; the sheet of copy paper in the machine is not as hard to face as we feared. Sometimes a love letter writes itself, and we love Ross so, and bear him such respect, that these quick notes, which purport to record the sorrow that runs through here and dis-

---

*Harold Ross founded *The New Yorker* in 1925 and was editor until his death. Katharine and E. B. White maintained a close personal friendship with Ross in addition to working with him at the magazine.

solves so many people, cannot possibly seem overstated or silly. Ross, even on this terrible day, is a hard man to keep quiet; he obtrudes—his face, his voice, his manner, even his amused interest in the critical proceedings. If he were accorded the questionable privilege of stopping by here for a few minutes, he would gorge himself on the minor technical problems that a magazine faces when it must do something in a hurry and against some sort of odds—in this case, emotional ones of almost overpowering weight. He would be far more interested in the grinding of the machinery than in what was being said about him.

All morning, people have wandered in and out of our cell, some tearfully, some guardedly, some boisterously, most of them long-time friends in various stages of repair. We have amused ourself thinking of Ross's reaction to this flow. "Never bother a writer" was one of his strongest principles. He used to love to drop in, himself, and sit around, but was uneasy the whole time because of the carking feeling that if only he would get up and go away, we might settle down to work and produce something. To him, a writer at work, whether in the office or anywhere in the outside world, was an extraordinarily interesting, valuable, but fragile object; and he half expected it to fall into a thousand pieces at any moment.

The report of Ross's death came over the telephone in a three-word sentence that somehow managed to embody all the faults that Ross devoted his life to correcting. A grief-stricken friend in Boston, charged with the task of spreading the news but too dazed to talk sensibly, said, "It's all over." He meant that Ross was dead, but the listener took it to mean that the operation was over. Here, in three easy words, were the ambiguity, the euphemistic softness, the verbal infirmity that Harold W. Ross spent his life thrusting at. Ross regarded every sentence as the enemy, and believed that if a man watched closely enough, he would discover the vulnerable spot, the essential weakness. He devoted his life to making the weak strong—a rather specialized form of blood transfusion, to be sure, but one that he believed in with such a consuming passion that his spirit infected others and inspired them, and lifted them. Whatever it was, this contagion, this vapor in these marshes, it spread. None escaped it. Nor is it likely to be dissipated in a hurry.

His ambition was to publish one good magazine, not a string

of successful ones, and he thought of *The New Yorker* as a sort of movement. He came equipped with not much knowledge and only two books—Webster's Dictionary and Fowler's "Modern English Usage." These books were his history, his geography, his literature, his art, his music, his everything. Some people found Ross's scholastic deficiencies quite appalling, and were not sure they had met the right man. But he was the right man, and the only question was whether the other fellow was capable of being tuned to Ross's vibrations. Ross had a thing that is at least as good as, and sometimes better than, knowledge: he had a sort of natural drive in the right direction, plus a complete respect for the work and ideas and opinions of others. It took a little while to get on to the fact that Ross, more violently than almost anybody, was proceeding in a good direction, and carrying others along with him, under torrential conditions. He was like a boat being driven at the mercy of some internal squall, a disturbance he himself only half understood, and of which he was at times suspicious.

In a way, he was a lucky man. For a monument he has the magazine to date—one thousand three hundred and ninety-nine issues, born in the toil and pain that can be appreciated only by those who helped in the delivery room. These are his. They stand, unchangeable and open for inspection. We are, of course, not in a position to estimate the monument, even if we were in the mood to. But we are able to state one thing unequivocally: Ross set up a great target and pounded himself to pieces trying to hit it square in the middle. His dream was a simple dream; it was pure and had no frills: he wanted the magazine to be good, to be funny, and to be fair.

We say he was lucky. Some people cordially disliked him. Some were amused but not impressed. And then, last, there are the ones we have been seeing today, the ones who loved him and had him for a friend—people he looked after, and who looked after him. These last are the ones who worked close enough to him, and long enough with him, to cross over the barrier reef of noisy shallows that ringed him, into the lagoon that was Ross himself—a rewarding, and even enchanting, and relatively quiet place, utterly trustworthy as an anchorage. Maybe these people had all the luck. The entrance wasn't always easy to find.

He left a note on our desk one day apropos of something that had pleased him in the magazine. The note simply said, "I am encouraged to go on." That is about the way we feel today, because of his contribution. We are encouraged to go on.

When you took leave of Ross, after a calm or stormy meeting, he always ended with the phrase that has become as much a part of the office as the paint on the walls. He would wave his limp hand, gesturing you away. "All right," he would say. "God bless you." Considering Ross's temperament and habits, this was a rather odd expression. He usually took God's name in vain if he took it at all. But when he sent you away with this benediction, which he uttered briskly and affectionately, and in which he and God seemed all scrambled together, it carried a warmth and sincerity that never failed to carry over. The words are so familiar to his helpers and friends here that they provide the only possible way to conclude this hasty notice and to take our leave. We cannot convey his manner. But with much love in our heart, we say, for everybody, "All right, Ross. God bless you!"

JAMES THURBER

11/11/61

I AM ONE OF THE LUCKY ONES: I knew him before blindness hit him, before fame hit him, and I tend always to think of him as a young artist in a small office in a big city, with all the world still ahead. It was a fine thing to be young and at work in New York for a new magazine when Thurber was young and at work, and I will always be glad that this happened to me.

It was fortunate that we got on well; the office we shared was the size of a hall bedroom. There was just room enough for two men, two typewriters, and a stack of copy paper. The copy paper disappeared at a scandalous rate—not because our production was high (although it was) but because Thurber used copy paper as the natural receptacle for discarded sorrows, immediate joys, stale dreams, golden prophecies, and messages of good cheer to the outside world and to fellow-workers. His mind was never at rest, and his pencil was connected to his mind by the best conductive tissue I have ever seen in action. The whole world knows what a funny man he was, but you had to sit next to him day after day to understand the extravagance of his clowning, the wildness and subtlety of his thinking, and the intensity of his interest in others and his sympathy for their dilemmas—dilemmas that he instantly enlarged, put in focus, and made immortal, just as he enlarged and made immortal the strange goings on in the Ohio home of his boyhood. His waking dreams and his sleeping dreams commingled shamelessly and uproariously. Ohio was never far from his thoughts, and when he received a medal from his home state in 1953, he wrote, "The clocks that strike in my dreams are often the clocks of Columbus." It is a beautiful sentence and a revealing one.

He was both a practitioner of humor and a defender of it. The day he died, I came on a letter from him, dictated to a secretary and signed in pencil with his sightless and enormous "Jim." "Every time is a time for humor," he wrote. "I write humor the way a surgeon operates, because it is a livelihood, because I have a great urge to do it, because many interesting challenges are set up, and because I have the hope it may do some good." Once, I remember, he heard someone say that humor is a shield, not a sword, and it made him mad. He wasn't going to have anyone beating his sword into a shield. That "surgeon," incidentally, is pure Mitty. During his happiest years, Thurber did not write the way a surgeon operates, he wrote the way a child skips rope, the way a mouse waltzes.

Although he is best known for "Walter Mitty" and "The Male Animal," the book of his I like best is "The Last Flower." In it you will find his faith in the renewal of life, his feeling for the beauty and fragility of life on earth. Like all good writers, he fashioned his own best obituary notice. Nobody else can add to the record, much as he might like to. And of all the flowers, real and figurative, that will find their way to Thurber's last resting place, the one that will remain fresh and wiltproof is the little flower he himself drew, on the last page of that lovely book.

JOHN F. KENNEDY

11/30/63

WHEN WE THINK OF HIM, he is without a hat, standing in the wind and the weather. He was impatient of topcoats and hats, preferring to be exposed, and he was young enough and tough enough to confront and to enjoy the cold and the wind of these times, whether the winds of nature or the winds of political circumstance and national danger. He died of exposure, but in a way that he would have settled for—in the line of duty, and with his friends and enemies all around, supporting him and shooting at him. It can be said of him, as of few men in a like position, that he did not fear the weather, and did not trim his sails, but instead challenged the wind itself, to improve its direction and to cause it to blow more softly and more kindly over the world and its people.

SELECTIVE BIBLIOGRAPHY

I. PRIMARY SOURCES: E. B. WHITE

A. Books

Another Ho Hum: More Newsbreaks from The New Yorker. New York: Farrar, 1932.

Charlotte's Web. New York: Harper, 1952.

An E. B. White Reader. Ed. William W. Watt and Robert W. Bradford. New York: Harper, 1966.

The Elements of Style by William Strunk, Jr., and E. B. White. New York: Macmillan, 1959; 2nd rev., 1972; 3rd rev., 1979.

Essays of E. B. White. New York: Harper, 1977.

Every Day Is Saturday. New York: Harper, 1934. Ann Arbor: UMI, 1967.

Farewell to Model T by Lee Strout White [pseud.]. New York: Putnam's, 1936.

The Fox Of Peapack and Other Poems. New York: Harper, 1938. Ann Arbor: UMI, 1967.

Here Is New York. New York: Harper, 1949. New York: Warner, 1988.

Ho Hum: Newsbreaks from The New Yorker. New York: Farrar, 1931.

Is Sex Necessary? Or Why You Feel the Way You Do by James Thurber and E. B. White. New York: Harper, 1929. With new introduction by White, New York: Harper, 1950. White wrote the Foreword, Chapters 2, 4, 6, 8, "Answers to Hard Questions," and "A Note on the Drawings in this Book."

The Lady Is Cold: Poems by E. B. White. New York: Harper, 1929. Ann Arbor: UMI, 1967.

Letters of E. B. White. Ed. Dorothy Lobrano Guth. New York: Harper, 1976.

One Man's Meat. New York: Harper, 1942. *One Man's Meat: A New and Enlarged Edition.* New York: Harper, 1944. *One Man's Meat.* With Introduction by Morris Bishop, New York: Harper, 1950; with Introduction by Walter Blair, New York: Harper, 1964; with Introduction by E. B. White, New York: Harper, 1983.

Poems and Sketches of E. B. White. New York: Harper, 1981.

The Points of My Compass: Letters from the East, the West, the North, the South. New York: Harper, 1962.

Quo Vadimus? Or the Case for the Bicycle. New York: Harper, 1939. Freeport, NY: Books for Libraries, 1972.

The Second Tree from the Corner. New York: Harper, 1954; with "E. B. White: An Appreciation" by William W. Watt, New York: Harper, 1962; with new introduction by E. B. White, New York: Harper, 1984.

Stuart Little. New York: Harper, 1945. *Stuart Little* [first five chapters]. Chicago: Science Research Associates, 1963. *Stuart Little in the Schoolroom* [12th chapter of *Stuart Little*]. New York: Harper, 1962.

The Trumpet of the Swan. New York: Harper, 1970.

The Wild Flag: Editorials from The New Yorker *on Federal World Government and Other Matters.* Boston: Houghton, 1946. Ann Arbor: UMI, 1967.

B. Other Books Edited or with Contributions by White

"E. B. White." *More Junior Authors.* Ed. Muriel Fuller. New York: Wilson, 1963, pp. 225–26.

Foreword. The New Yorker *Album.* Garden City, NY: Doubleday, 1928.

Foreword. *The Second* New Yorker *Album.* Garden City, NY: Doubleday, 1929.

Foreword. *The Third* New Yorker *Album.* Garden City, NY: Doubleday, 1930.

Four Freedoms. Ed. E. B. White. Washington, DC: Office of War Information, 1942.

"I'd Send My Son to Cornell." *Our Cornell.* Comp. Raymond F. Howes. Ithaca, NY: Cayuga, 1939, pp. 11–18. Reprinted in *The College Years.* Ed. A. C. Spectorsky. New York: Hawthorn, 1958, pp. 464–67.

Introduction. *A Basic Chicken Guide for the Small Flock Owner* by Roy E. Jones. New York: Morrow, 1944, pp. v–viii.

Introduction. *The Lives and Times of Archy & Mehitabel* by Don Marquis. Garden City, NY: Doubleday, 1950, pp. xvii–xxiv.

Introduction. *Onward and Upward in the Garden* by Katharine S. White. New York: Farrar, 1979, pp. vii–xix.

Introduction. *The Owl in the Attic* by James Thurber. New York: Harper, 1931, pp. xi–xvi.

Introduction. *Spider, Egg, and Microcosm: Three Men and Three Worlds of Science* by Eugene Kinkead. New York: Knopf, 1955, pp. v–vii.

[Letter]. *The Pied Pipers: Interviews with the Influential Creators of Children's Literature* by Justin Wintle and Emma Fisher. New York: Paddington, 1974, pp. 126–31.

Preface. *E. B. White: A Bibliographic Catalogue of Printed Materials in the Department of Rare Books, Cornell University Library.* Comp. Katherine Romans Hall. New York: Garland, 1979, pp. ix–x.

"Ross, Harold Wallace." *Encyclopaedia Britannica,* 1964 ed.

A Subtreasury of American Humor. Ed. E. B. White and Katharine S. White. New York: Coward, 1941.

"A Teaching Trinity." *The Teacher.* Ed. Morris Ernst. Englewood Cliffs, NJ: Prentice, 1967, pp. 103–05.

"Walden—A Young Man in Search of Himself" and "Concerning Henry Thoreau/1817–1862." *Walden* by Henry David Thoreau. Boston: Houghton, 1964, pp. vii–xvi.

C. Articles

For a listing of 2,190 articles White contributed to periodicals, see *E. B. White: A Bibliographic Catalogue of Printed Material in the Department of Rare Books, Cornell University Library.* Comp. Katherine Romans Hall. New York: Garland, 1979. This is the definitive bibliography of E. B. White's books and articles.

D. Collections

E. B. White's papers are held by the Department of Rare Books and Manuscripts, Cornell University Library, Ithaca, New York. The collection contains approximately 2,350 printed items; 1,275 manuscripts; 3,491 letters by White; 23,384 letters to White; and 5,500 related items such as clippings, photographs, films, and tapes. Researchers must obtain permission from White's son Joel to study the correspondence (requests addressed to the Department of Rare Books will be forwarded for his consideration). Katharine S. White's papers are held by Special Collections, Bryn Mawr College Library, Bryn Mawr, Pennsylvania.

American Literary Manuscripts lists twenty-six other depositories together holding five manuscripts, 75 letters by White, and 19 letters to White: Wesleyan University, Yale University, the Library of Congress, Knox College, Boston University, Harvard University, Colby College, the University of Michigan, the University of Minnesota, the State University of New York at Buffalo, Hamilton and Kirkland College, American Academy of Arts and Letters (NY), Columbia University, Pierpont Morgan Library (NY), Dartmouth College, Princeton University, Ohio State University, State Library of Pennsylvania, Haverford College, Pennsylvania State University, the University of Pennsylvania, the University of Texas, Randolph–Macon Woman's College, Middlebury College, the University of Vermont, and the University of Wyoming.

The *National Union Catalog of Manuscript Collections* lists two additional depositories with letters either to or by White: the University of Illinois (Stanley White papers) and the Newberry Library in Chicago (Dale Kramer papers). Dorothy G. Lobrano in *Letters of E. B. White* indicates three more depositories with White letters: Stanford University, New York University, and the New York Public Library. A. J. Anderson in *E. B. White: A Bibliography* indicates that the New York Public Library at Lincoln Center has a typescript of a White play, "The Firebug's Homecoming." Library of Congress collections that should have letters to or by White include those of Henry F. Pringle, Irita Van Doren, James M.

Cain, Janet Flanner, and Frederick L. Allen. Three other collections at Cornell besides the White collection should contain letters to or by White: the papers of Bristow Adams, Romeyn Berry, and Morris G. Bishop.

II. Secondary Sources: E. B. White

A. Bibliographies

Anderson, A. J. *E. B. White: A Bibliography.* Metuchen, NJ: Scarecrow, 1978. (This bibliography is particularly useful for its listings of secondary sources, such as book reviews of White's books.)

Hall, Katherine Romans, comp. *E. B. White: A Bibliographic Catalogue of Printed Materials in the Department of Rare Books, Cornell University Library.* New York: Garland, 1979. (This bibliography gives detailed information on each of White's books and identifies White's articles in periodicals, often by indicating from which words to which words are White's. No secondary sources are included.)

B. Biographical Items

Bacon, Leonard. "Humors and Careers." *Saturday Review of Literature* 29 Apr 1939: 3–4, 22.

Benet, Laura. *Famous English and American Essayists.* New York: Dodd, 1966, pp. 119–22.

Collins, David R. *To the Point: A Story about E. B. White.* Minneapolis: Carolrhoda, 1989. (Written for children.)

Elledge, Scott. *E. B. White: A Biography.* New York: Norton, 1985.

Thurber, James. "E. B. W." *Saturday Review of Literature* 15 Oct 1938: 8–9. Reprinted in *Saturday Review Gallery.* Ed. Jerome Beatty, Jr. New York: Simon, 1957, pp. 302–07.

Updike, John. "Remarks on the Occasion of E. B. White's Receiving the 1971 National Medal for Literature, 12/2/71." *Picked-Up Pieces.* New York: Knopf, 1975, pp. 434–47.

C. Interviews

[Lee, Bruce]. "Typewriter Man." *Newsweek* 22 Feb 1960: 72.

Mitgang, Herbert. "Down East with E. B. White." *New York Times* 17 Nov 1976: C19.

Nordell, Roderick. "The Writer as a Private Man." *Christian Science Monitor* 31 Oct 1962: 9.

Plimpton, George A., and Frank H. Crowther. "The Art of the Essay, I: E. B. White." *Paris Review* 48 (1969): 65–88.

Shenker, Israel. "E. B. White: Notes and Comment by Author." *New York Times* 11 Jul 1969: 37, 43.

van Gelder, Robert. "An Interview with Mr. E. B. White, Essayist." *New York Times Book Review* 2 Aug 1942: 2. Reprinted in *Writers and*

Writing by Robert Van Gelder. New York: Scribner's, 1946, pp. 308–10.

D. Critical Studies (Works for Adults)

Beck, Warren. "E. B. White." *English Journal* 35 (1946): 175–81.

Blair, Walter, and Hamlin Hill. "White and Thurber." *America's Humor: From Poor Richard to Doonesbury.* New York: Oxford University Press, 1978, pp. 437–47.

Core, George. "The Eloquence of Fact." *Virginia Quarterly Review* 54 (1978): 733–41.

Cox, Richard. "Nonfiction in the Classroom: E. B. White's 'Once More to the Lake.' " *Conference of College Teachers of English Studies* 52 (1987): 20–27.

Enright, D. J. "Laurel—or Brussels Sprouts?" *Encounter* Apr 1978: 70–75. Reprinted as "Lifting Up One's Life a Trifle: On E. B. White." *A Mania for Sentences.* London: Chatto, 1983, pp. 185–92.

Epstein, Joseph. "E. B. White, Dark and Lite." *Commentary* Apr 1986: 48–56. Reprinted in *Partial Payments: Essays on Writers and Their Lives.* New York: Norton, 1989, pp. 295–319.

Fadiman, Clifton. "In Praise of E. B. White, Realist." *New York Times Book Review* 10 June 1945: 1, 10, 12, 14–16. Reprinted in *Reading, Living and Thinking.* Eds. J. R. Chamberlain, W. B. Pressy, and R. E. Waters. New York: Scribner's, 1948, pp. 180–91. Reprinted in *Symposium.* Ed. G. W. Arms and L. G. Locke. New York: Rinehart, 1954, pp. 329–35.

Fuller, John Wesley. *Prose Styles in the Essays of E. B. White.* Dissertation, University of Washington, 1959. Ann Arbor: UMI, 1979.

Grant, Thomas. "The Sparrow on the Ledge: E. B. White in New York." *Studies in American Humor* ns 3 (1984): 24–33.

Haskell, Dale Everett. *The Rhetoric of the Familiar Essay: E. B. White and Personal Discourse.* Dissertation, Texas Christian University, 1983. Ann Arbor: UMI, 1983. DEQ-07824.

Hasley, Louis. "The Talk of the Town and the Country: E. B. White." *Connecticut Review* Oct 1971: 37–45.

Heldreth, Leonard G. " 'Pattern of Life Indelible': E. B. White's 'Once More to the Lake.' " *CEA Critic* 45 (1982): 31–34.

Howarth, William. "E. B. White at *The New Yorker.*" *Sewanee Review* 93 (1985): 574–83.

Lang, Berel. "Strunk and White and Grammar as Morality." *Soundings* 65 (1982): 23–30.

Martin, Edward A. "Out of the World of Nonsense: Ring Lardner, Frank Sullivan, and E. B. White." *H. L. Mencken and the Debunkers.* Athens: University of Georgia Press, 1984, pp. 157–76.

Platizky, Roger S. " 'Once More to the Lake': A Mythic Interpretation." *College Literature* 15 (1988): 171–79.

Rogers, Barbara. "E. B. White." *American Writers: A Collection of Literary Biographies*, Supplement I, Part 2. New York: Scribner's, 1979, pp. 651–81.

Sampson, Edward. *E. B. White*. New York: Twayne, 1974.

———. "E. B. White." *American Humorists, 1800–1950*. Ed. Stanley Trachtenberg. Dictionary of Literary Biography Vol. 11. Detroit: Gale, 1982, 2: 568–83.

Steinhoff, William R. " 'The Door,' 'The Professor,' 'My Friend the Poet (Deceased),' 'The Washable House,' and 'The Man Out in Jersey.' " *College English* 23 (1961): 229–32.

Warshow, Robert S. "E. B. White and *The New Yorker.*" *Movies, Comics, Theatre & Other Aspects of Popular Culture*. New York: Doubleday, 1962, pp. 105–08.

Yates, Norris. "E. B. White, 'Farmer/Other.' " *The American Humorist: Conscience of the Twentieth Century*. Ames: Iowa State University Press, 1964, pp. 299–320.

E. Critical Studies (Works for Children)

Apseloff, Marilyn. "*Charlotte's Web:* Flaws in the Weaving." *Children's Novels and the Movies*. Ed. Douglas Street. New York: Ungar, 1983, pp. 171–81.

Gagnon, Laurence. "Webs of Concern: *The Little Prince* and *Charlotte's Web.*" *Children's Literature: The Great Excluded*. Ed. Francelia Butler. Storrs, CT: Children's Literature Association, 1973, 2: 61–66.

Glastonbury, Marion. "E. B. White's Unexpected Items of Enchantment." *Children's Literature in Education* May 1973: 3–11.

Griffith, John. "Charlotte's Web: A Lonely Fantasy of Love." *Children's Literature* 8 (1980): 111–17.

Kinghorn, Norton D. "The Real Miracle of *Charlotte's Web.*" *Children's Literature Association Quarterly* 11 (1986): 4–9.

Landes, S. E. B. "White's *Charlotte's Web:* Caught in the Web." *Touchstones: Reflections on the Best in Children's Literature*. Ed. Perry Nodelman. West Lafayette, IN: Children's Literature Association, 1985, pp. 270–80.

Nodelman, Perry. "Text as Teacher: The Beginning of *Charlotte's Web.*" *Children's Literature* 13 (1985): 109–27.

Neumeyer, Peter F. "The Creation of *Charlotte's Web:* From Drafts to Book." *Horn Book* Oct 1982: 489–97; Dec 1982: 617–25.

———. "The Creation of E. B. White's *The Trumpet of the Swan:* The Manuscripts." *Horn Book* Jan/Feb 1985: 17. (Condensed from paper presented at University of North Carolina.)

———. "What Makes a Good Children's Book? The Texture of *Charlotte's Web.*" *South Atlantic Bulletin* May 1979: 66–75.

Rees, David. "Timor Mortis Conturbat Me: E. B. White and Doris Buchanan Smith." *The Marble in the Water: Essays on Contemporary*

Writers of Fiction for Children and Young Adults. Boston: Horn Book, 1980, pp. 68–77.

Sale, Roger. *Fairy Tales and After: From Snow White to E. B. White.* Cambridge, MA: Harvard University Press, 1978.

Shohet, Richard M. *Functions of Voice in Children's Literature.* Dissertation, Harvard University, 1971. Ann Arbor: UMI, 1971, 72-00297.

Solheim, Helene. "Magic in the Web: Time, Pigs, and E. B. White." *South Atlantic Quarterly* 80 (1981): 391–405.

Weales, Gerald. "The Designs of E. B. White." *Authors and Illustrators of Children's Books: Writings on Their Lives and Works.* Ed. Miriam Hoffman and Eva Samuels. New York: Bowker, 1972, pp. 409–10.

Welty, Eudora. "E. B. White's *Charlotte's Web.*" *The Eye of the Story: Selected Essays and Reviews.* New York: Random, 1978, pp. 203–06.

III. SECONDARY SOURCES: RELATED SUBJECTS

A. Katharine S. White

Davis, Linda H. *Onward and Upward: A Biography of Katharine S. White.* New York: Harper, 1987.

Nerney, Brian James. *Katharine S. White,* New Yorker *Editor: Her Influence on the* New Yorker *and on American Literature.* Dissertation, University of Minnesota, 1982. Ann Arbor, UMI, 1982, DEP 83-08103.

B. James Thurber

Burnstein, Burton. *Thurber: A Biography.* New York: Dodd, 1975.

Holmes, Charles S. *The Clocks of Columbus: The Literary Career of James Thurber.* New York: Atheneum, 1972.

Thurber, Helen, and Edward Weeks, eds. *Selected Letters of James Thurber.* Boston: Little, 1980.

Toombs, Sarah Eleanora. *James Thurber: An Annotated Bibliography of Criticism.* New York: Garland, 1987.

C. Harold Ross

Churchill, Allen. "Ross of the *New Yorker.*" *American Mercury* Aug 1948: 147–55.

Grant, Jane. *Ross,* The New Yorker, *and Me.* New York: Reynal, 1968.

Kramer, Dale. *Ross and* The New Yorker. New York: Doubleday, 1951.

Kramer, Dale, and George R. Clark. "Harold Ross and *The New Yorker.*" *Harper's* Apr 1943: 510–21.

Rovere, Richard H. "The Magnificent Fussbudget." *Harper's* Jun 1975: 97–100.

Thurber, James. *The Years with Ross.* Boston: Little, 1959.

D. Other Items on The New Yorker

Bone, Martha Denham. *Dorothy Parker and* New Yorker *Satire.* Dissertation, Middle Tennessee State University, 1985. Ann Arbor: UMI, 1985, DES 85-23970.

Gill, Brendan. *Here at* The New Yorker. New York: Random, 1975.

Houghton, Donald Eugene. The New Yorker: *Exponent of a Cosmopolitan Elite.* Dissertation, University of Minnesota, 1955. Ann Arbor: UMI, 1955, 00-13784.

[Ingersoll, Ralph.] *"The New Yorker." Fortune* Aug 1934: 72–86, 90, 92, 97, 150, 152.

Kahn, Ely Jacques. *About* The New Yorker *and Me: A Sentimental Journal.* New York: Putnam, 1979.

Kramer, Hilton. "Harold Ross's *New Yorker." Commentary* Aug 1959: 122–27.

Maloney, Russell. "Tilley the Toiler." *Saturday Review of Literature* Aug 1947: 7–10, 29–32.

Morton, Charles W. "A Try for *The New Yorker"* and "Brief Interlude at *The New Yorker." Atlantic Monthly* Apr 1963: 45–49; May 1963: 81–85.

Rouit, Earl. "Modernism and Three Magazines: An Editorial Revolution." *Sewanee Review* 93 (1985): 540–53.

Studies in American Humor ns 3 (1984): 7–97 (special issue: The New Yorker *From 1925 to 1950*).

Weales, Gerald. "Not for the Old Lady in Dubuque." *The Comic Imagination in American Literature.* Ed. Louis D. Rubin, Jr. New Brunswick: Rutgers University Press, 1973, pp. 231–46.